W9-CPV-763

The Private Gardens of Charleston

LOUISA PRINGLE CAMERON

The Private Gardens of Charleston

WYRICK & COMPANY

Published by Wyrick & Company
Post Office Box 89
Charleston, South Carolina 29402

Set in Berkeley Old Style by Crane Typesetting Service, Inc.
Printed and bound by Everbest Printing Co.
Ltd., China
Designed by Sandra Strother Hudson

Library of Congress Cataloging-in-Publication Data
Cameron, Louisa Pringle, 1953–
The private gardens of Charleston / Louisa Pringle Cameron.
p.   cm.
Includes bibliographical references.
ISBN 0-941711-14-5 : $39.95
1. Gardens—South Carolina—Charleston.   2. Gardens—South
Carolina—Charleston—Pictorial works.   3. Charleston (S.C.)—
Description.   I. Title.
SB466.U65C533   1991
712'.6'09757915—dc20   *91-10251*
                                                          CIP

Frontispiece: The garden of the William Gibbes House.
Photograph by Terry Richardson.

This book is dedicated to the memory of my grandfather
DANIEL ELLIOTT HUGER
who instilled in me a love of gardening at an early age
and to my mother
LOUISE HUGER PRINGLE
who has given so much love and support for all my endeavors

"It is difficult indeed to write of an old Charleston garden apart from the house, for the two have long been intimates, and the grace of the garden, the fragrance of years of roses, has lent a poignant sweetness to the grave dignity of the mansion, which for more than a century has stretched walls like protecting arms about the garden's loveliness; while the repose of the house, born of the rare qualities of nobility of proportion, of harmony, of balance, has dowered the garden with something of its own serenity, its memories, its unvexed quietness."

Frances Duncan, *Century Magazine,* 1907

 *Contents*

⚜ *Acknowledgements* ⚜

Most of the credit for this book belongs to the talented, creative gardeners and owners for their patience, kindness, enthusiasm, and ongoing interest in gardening. Their Herculean efforts to put their gardens back in order after Hurricane Hugo are noteworthy.

In addition, several individuals made special efforts to help. I am indebted to my publisher and editor, Pete Wyrick, for his steady encouragement, support, and belief in the final product. Without his gentle guidance, I would never have discovered and pursued the art of photography.

I am extremely grateful to Tom Blagden, Jr. for his superb guidance and advice on photographing the gardens. His recently published *Lowcountry, The Natural Landscape* was inspirational. The staffs at the Charleston Library Society, The South Carolina Historical Society, and The Charleston Museum library were constantly helpful.

A very special thank-you goes to Cindy Byrns, who cheerfully put in many hours to type the rough drafts and manuscript. Elaine Hartley deserves thanks for typing numerous "finals." Roberta Kefalos, editor and publicist at Wyrick & Company, was instrumental in helping me through the final stages; her sharp-minded ideas and comments were invaluable. Kate Adams was likewise an astute proofreader.

Finally, throughout the whole endeavor, my husband, Price, was an ardent supporter and a kind, but perceptive critic. My son, Price, always enthusiastic, fended for himself without complaint, when necessary. To them and to the many friends who helped, encouraged, inquired, lent books and gave advice, thank you.

❧ *Introduction* ☙

In the spring of 1989, my husband and I opened our garden to the public for the first time, during the Historic Charleston Foundation's Annual Festival of Houses and Gardens. An enthusiastic visitor from Texas asked what books she could take home on Charleston's private gardens. I answered that the only one I was familiar with was *Charleston Gardens*, by Loutrel Briggs (1893–1977), but that it had been published in the early 1950's and was out of print. She shrugged, gave me a piercing look, and asked, "Why don't you write a new one?" And so the seed was sown and from it grew *The Private Gardens of Charleston*.

This book does not attempt to educate the reader about the history of Charleston gardens, for many of them are quite well-documented, especially the famous trio near the city: Middleton, Magnolia, and Cypress Gardens. Plats of some seventeenth- and eighteenth-century city gardens can be found on early tax maps. Mrs. Emma Richardson published charming pamphlets for the Charleston Museum on early plats and on the garden at the Heyward-Washington House on Church Street, describing typical flowers of the period. On the same subject, Miss Elise Pinckney wrote a fascinating account of Thomas and Elizabeth Lamboll, two early Charleston gardeners, also published for the Museum. Thomas Lamboll's correspondence with the famous eighteenth-century botanist, John Bartram, gives an idea of the tradition of enthusiasm for research, collecting, and growing plant material that started with the earliest explorations of the Lowcountry.

In his introduction to *Charleston Gardens*, Loutrel Briggs provides historical and botanical backgrounds for gardening in the Lowcountry, noting such famous residents and visitors as Dr. Alexander Garden, for whom the fragrant gardenia was named; André Michaux, sent by the French government to collect specimens for the royal plantations; and Joel R. Poinsett, who described the red flowers of the poinsettia, seen in Mexico in 1833.

In addition to his significant documentation of gardens in and near the city, the late Mr. Briggs made an enduring contribution to the architecture and landscape of the area in the middle of this century. Records show that he worked with the owners of over one hundred and fifteen gardens downtown and in neighboring subdivisions. His associate, Mary Mikell Barnwell, was responsible for several well-known designs. A native of New York City and a landscape architect, Mr. Briggs came to Charleston in 1927 to help design the gardens at Mepkin, Mulberry, and Rice Hope plantations. He became a winter resident, frequently residing at the Brewton Inn, where he gave lectures on southern gardening. A 1931 publication described a course of study covering the following topics: general principles of garden design; identification of southern plants; southern plants for winter effect; and a field lecture on plants in Charleston gardens. In 1959, he became a permanent resident and designed a lovely garden for his wife behind their house on Ladson Street.

In addition to his book, Mr. Briggs occasionally wrote articles expressing strong views on plant material and design. He preferred having gardens visible and accessible from the living room rather than the kitchen, and he recognized the special complications of small, irregular lots. An article in a 1941 edition of *The News and Courier* quotes his opinion on garden trends: "The average American garden now is less architectural than the Italian, not so stiffly patterned as the French nor so abundantly planted as the English. We are developing a distinct type, following the English precedent more than any other, which is a happy combination of architectual quality and planting design." This "happy combination" is precisely what Mr. Briggs accomplished in garden after garden, complementing the distinctive architecture of Charleston's houses as well as the lifestyles of the owners.

Tastes in gardens, as in interior decoration, shift over the years, often reflecting the current needs of

xiii

these extensions of our living spaces. Many "yards" go through long spells of hard use by children and pets, only to blossom forth for a while before repeating the cycle. A change in ownership can mean neglect or glory. Charleston has lost untold numbers of gardens to wars, storms, extreme weather, earthquakes, fires, development, and even restoration. But change is the hallmark of a garden; it represents the bitter and the sweet. Constant, inevitable disappointments are assuaged by spring's promise of splendor, summer's lush growth, fall's subtlety and surprises, winter's calm. Maturity of gardens is a factor in change; some flowering fruit trees, for example, live only twenty or thirty years. Large trees spread over previously sunny spaces, resulting in areas that eventually need to be treated as shade gardens or otherwise altered drastically.

Over the past ten years a revival in gardening interest has led to the creation and restoration of an increasing number of gardens. The most recent change, however, was due to Hurricane Hugo, which roared into Charleston on Thursday, September 21, 1989. Thousands of trees were ripped, toppled, and uprooted. Entire gardens were inundated with salt water during the tidal surge. Walls, fences, and gates were damaged. Three months following the storm, a hard freeze hit the city, along with the first snowfall ever recorded at Christmas. Indomitably, Charlestonians began the long process of recovery, re-roofing their houses and replanting their gardens.

Our temperate climate is highly conducive to growth. The average annual temperature range is 74° maximum, 57° minimum, although summers are hot and humid. The average growing season is 294 days; December 10 is the average date of the first freeze, and February 19 is the last. Temperatures below 20°

and over 100° are considered unusual. The average rainfall is about 48 inches a year.

The Cooperative Extension Service of Clemson University provides a wealth of information on gardening in Charleston County and has publications available on every subject from azaleas to the trace mineral zinc. It also offers a Master Gardener program whose graduates will help answer gardening questions during the week. The local garden centers and plant nurseries (both retail and wholesale) are extremely helpful. An index listing botanical and common names for much of the plant material mentioned in this book is included in the appendix.

The choice of plant material is often restricted by the limitations of city lots. Narrow, shady walks and driveways, high walls, and small spaces require certain concessions, as does the desire for privacy. Even the much-despised and invasive cherry laurel may be allowed to flourish if its evergreen leaves protect a view from (or of) a neighboring house. On the other hand, a common wall or facade may be an important focal point.

The settings of the gardens are given much thought and attention, for they are frequently the scenes of cocktail parties, wedding receptions, luncheons, dinners, and children's birthday parties. Shaded seating areas are desirable, as is off-street parking, and both spaces are well incorporated into these gardens. Most of the gardens have entrances from the street and boast a delightful array of wrought iron and wooden gates.

The variety of the gardens pictured herein is testament not only to the rich horticultural and architectural history of Charleston, but also to the creativity and talent of its many gardeners, landscape architects, and garden designers, past and present.

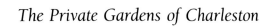

The Private Gardens of Charleston

The Garden of the James Huston House

Years before this property fell into the gifted hands of its present owners, the venerable Charleston author, Samuel G. Stoney, described it as having a "charming walled garden" on what was probably part of the original plat of the Planter's Hotel, now the Dock Street Theatre.

Paved in old brick and totally enclosed by high walls, the garden is a delightful extension of the handsome 1809 residence, which was once used as a shop. The street door is false, for the actual entryway is to the south, via a brick and pebble driveway, and is framed by a fragrant arch of Confederate jasmine. A scooped white picket gate marks the entrance to a series of courtyards.

When Mr. and Mrs. Joseph McGee bought the house twenty-five years ago, an adjacent roofless building was part of the parcel. Largely ignored, it remained while plans proceeded for building a much-needed extension behind the original house.

"We loved the idea of a living space which completely opened to the outside, and we designed the room accordingly. I was strongly influenced by the compact garden designed by landscape architect Robert Marvin for the C & S Bank 'Pink House' on Queen Street, and worked out a plan for our main courtyard where we could breakfast and enjoy company on pretty evenings. But gardening in a small space was difficult. The environment was completely different from the gardening I grew up with—azaleas under the filtered shade of tall pines, open spaces, sunny spring borders. Because of the dense shade cast by neighboring buildings, trees and walls, my garden was all green with just a few bright pots of geraniums. It was an effort just controlling the rampant fig vine (*Ficus pumila*) that covered the ten-foot walls.

"One day, a gardener friend advised, 'You've just *got* to get rid of that vine.' So we spent a day doing some judicious pruning. A week later, to our horror, the entire three-story south facade of the Dock Street Theatre was an unsightly mass of dead vines—and the Spoleto Festival was in full swing!"

During Spoleto, a major, international arts festival that takes place in Charleston every May and June, the garden is the site of daily activity. In 1977, the first year of the Festival, the McGees invited the musicians for light refreshments after the midday chamber concerts at the Dock Street Theatre. "This had always been a part of tradition in the town of Spoleto, Italy, and it has become a tradition with us that greatly enriches our lives," says Mrs. McGee.

With entertaining in mind, it was decided that more space was needed, so in 1985, landscape architects Hugh and Mary Palmer Dargan were consulted.

"We wanted to connect a garage/potting shed behind our roofless ruin with the rest of the property," explains Mrs. McGee. "Inside the shell of the empty building was a side yard with a little grass, some bulbs for cutting and the remnants of a play yard for the children, complete with sandbox and swing set. But we did not want to tear down the walls and lose the intimacy of separate courtyard 'rooms' by creating one large space, so portions were reinforced with steel beams and entrance arches were repaired and created. With the help of Hugo Tezza, a talented mason, the entire area was paved; low brick walls defined a fountain and beds around the perimeter, while latticework disguised the garage and gave support for climbers. It was important to save a lovely old Lady Banks rose, and Mary Palmer Dargan suggested an arbor which could span the narrow space between the house and the retaining wall of the salvaged old building.

"The planting was all mine," notes Mrs. McGee. "It was, and still is, a labor of love, but the only way I will really learn about plants is to try them. I probably break more rules than not, although in such a small space, I can easily replace mistakes. I treat the sunny beds almost like window boxes and constantly move around a large number of pots. The pots visu-

A flowering peach arches gracefully over the entrance to the James Huston House garden.

In the south courtyard, potted shrimp plant (*Justicia Brandegeana*), and an unusual variegated flowering maple highlight a corner with vibrant oranges and yellows. A Lady Banks rose spills over the wall.

other planters. Variegated ivies, ajuga, and *Vinca major* brighten the shadiest nooks and crannies. Ferns include asiatic, autumn, maidenhair, Japanese painted and leatherleaf varieties. The heavenly scent of jasmine pervades the entire courtyard off and on from late spring through early summer; *Clematis Armandii*, also showy, white, and fragrant, gracefully frames a doorway. Pink is a favorite in the garden; the cluster rose 'Maria Pavie' is combined with an unusual salmon-colored *Salvia coccinea*, deep pink foxgloves, and overflowing pots of double pale pink impatiens. The soft, neutral greys of dusty miller and santolina are expertly interspersed with more vibrant blossoms. The red of pineapple sage and the spectacular orange petals of an unusual flowering maple provide strong accents.

An inspired sense of scale, proportion, design and texture is evident at each turn. Against one wall, the

ally break up the surrounding brick and make it much easier to give the effect of color that I'd like to have in a larger garden. Containers also provide a means for vertical gardening, for brightening dark areas, and add a touch of whimsy."

Color is skillfully introduced among the hardy background plantings, which include hollies, fatsia, aucuba, jasmines, azaleas, camellias, nandina, holly ferns, and hydrangeas. Native columbine, bulbs, and pansies are planted for early spring, to be followed by begonias, impatiens, and wonderful arrangements of dianthus, alyssum, deep blue lobelia, dusty miller and heather in the numerous window boxes and

One of many carefully chosen wall ornaments.

4

Sunlight floods through a pergola, which spans a dining area between the house and one of its courtyards. The sculptural trunks distinguish mature Lady Banks roses.

A north courtyard frequently used for entertaining features a rich variety of textures, patterns and shade plants.

elegant bark of a camphor tree forms a backdrop for an equally elegant runner of small-leaf variegated ivy; triple miniature topiaries placed on top of a wall add interest to a neighbor's white stucco above; and in one corner, the eye is casually led upward along the lines of an espaliered sasanqua to a wall sculpture.

"Because the garden is so small," remarks Mrs. McGee, "I had to learn how to keep things in proportion. Friends are a great help and are always offering books, articles, and sometimes plants. One friend in particular, who worked at Callaway Gardens, brought Penelope Hobhouse to see the garden and then returned for a week's visit. She helped with pruning, which opened spaces, and offered encouragement for learning, planning, and experimenting with new plant material, especially perennials." A portable greenhouse comes out in the winter for tender specimens.

Creating solutions for problem areas is an enjoyable challenge. "I'm still looking for the perfect foun-

tain statue and have recently been inspired by a photograph to design a large wrought iron wall planter for a difficult space." Another project is to widen the bed along the western half of the driveway, which would allow for lusher and more vertical planting in that spot.

"I enjoy selecting plants for their foliage and like to arrange them in groups of three. If they don't work out or get too large, they are quickly given away or used in another location. I keep a journal of photographs from year to year and am trying to correctly label as much as possible. Trips to other gardens, lectures, and seminars are inspirational, as are the gardeners themselves. Clubs can help. Four years ago, ten of us started a small group so we could learn with each other. We recently sponsored a short course in landscape design.

"I keep very busy with the garden and find it a necessity to toil away daily, but it is such a joy in my life—it feeds my soul."

6

One of two doors opening into the courtyards from the garden room addition.

Behind the neat, three-story brick facade of this circa 1780 "tenement" building is a small courtyard entirely hidden from the street. The attainment of privacy, however, was gradual.

When Mr. and Mrs. James Conner purchased the property in 1927, the present garden was open to an alley. A dray still came through the dirt yard, delivering coal and wood to several houses. At the risk of offending neighbors, one of the Conners' first priorities was to enclose the yard with both an addition to the house and brick walls in place of short fences. Over the years, the height of the walls was increased to about ten feet.

Entering the garden from the house, a wrought iron gate leads onto an open, paved porch providing shade and sheltered access to parking. A second story screened porch overlooks the courtyard below.

Roughly square in plan, with a central circle of white azaleas surrounding a clipped conical yew, the courtyard is paved with old brick. Its most distinguishing feature is the tapestry-like effect produced by a variety of evergreen foliage plants arranged in the borders against the warm brick walls. Cleyera, loropetalum, two kinds of yew, fatsia, hollyfern, ligustrum, nandina, aucuba, tea olive, ivies, camellias, Florida anise, azaleas, holly, mahonia, and cedar have been skillfully grouped and carefully pruned. A loquat curves out over comfortable chaises and chairs placed within view of a small fountain where birds drink and splash. Begonias may add a touch of summer color, followed by camellias and chrysanthemums in the fall and winter and azaleas in the spring, but Mrs. Conner particularly enjoys the foliage. "I *love* green," she explains. "I have bought every shade of it, with every texture I could find, changing and moving things around from time to time, frequently bringing pots into the house. I have scores of plants inside, too, for if you take foliage out of a house, it no longer looks lived-in to me, and my all-green garden is certainly an extension of my living space."

Elaborating on the use of her courtyard, she points out a bar on the porch equipped for heating food. Buffet suppers and luncheons outside are a favorite form of entertainment. The courtyard is well-lit at night, and globed candles on stands provide additional soft lighting.

Several trees, including a Leyland cypress, photinia, Savannah hollies, and althea lend verticality and enhance the privacy of the garden. Help is necessary for maintenance, but Mrs. Conner enjoys doing as much of the digging, pruning, and clipping as she can, noting the pleasure it has given her and her friends over the years.

Above: A handsome shade-tolerant shrub is the anise tree (*Illicium floridanum*), which produces small but showy red flowers in early spring. A white variety is also available. *Top right:* White azaleas around a clipped yew form a dramatic focal point in the courtyard. *Bottom right:* A pruned pair of loropetalums in bloom flanks yew and fatsia, forming a tapestry of greens.

9

For approximately thirty years, from the late twenties through the early sixties, the two old brick buildings at Brewton's Corner on Church Street housed an inn and tea room. Loutrel Briggs was a frequent visitor, and he designed the property's only garden space, a courtyard, in 1927. A central fountain with a sundial was its main feature; shade was provided by a standard wisteria tree and a wisteria arbor. In springtime, it must have been heavenly to sip tea or coffee under those pendulous, fragrant clusters of bloom.

The focal point of the garden is its sundial fish pond. A protective ironwork cover was crafted locally and is removable.

Azaleas frame a statue in the predominantly white garden.

When the property was sold in 1985, one of the first priorities of the owners, Mr. & Mrs. Douglas B. Lee, was to restore the courtyard. A 1960's brick addition to the old storehouse/stable, which had been the tea room, encroached upon the edge of the fountain. The wisteria tree had long since disappeared, and the arbor had become the tiny garden of an adjacent dwelling. The first floor of the main house was being used as an antiques shop; stairs leading up from the courtyard provided access to living quarters.

Once the modern addition and its concrete slab foundation were demolished, the fountain again became the center of interest, and the large archway of the guest house was exposed. Removal of the outside stairs transformed the entrance view. The original paving slates were cracked beyond use, reinforcing the decision to put in a lawn. No salvageable plants remained, although a tangle of tenacious wisteria was excavated.

Brought up in Virginia, Mr. Lee was particularly fond of the ivy, brick, azaleas, and English box

Plantings of boxwood, holly, azaleas and tea olives are kept in scale with the proportions of this compact garden, formerly a paved courtyard. Ivy topiaries define corners of the lawn.

which reminded him of formal gardens in his native state. Two low brick walls separate the garden from neighbors. One was covered with ivy, and Mrs. Lee suggested clipping the unruly mess into neat swags, a motif which was successfully continued around two sides of the garden. Another success was their choice of a dwarf box hedge enclosing white azaleas. Hollies and standard clipped tea olives form the background, effectively creating three levels of planting. A tea olive brought from a previous garden had grown naturally into a standard, or tree form, inspiring its repetition.

Concerned about the dangerous attraction of a fish pond to children, the Lees asked Rick Avrett of Ole Charleston Forge to design a removable wrought iron cover. They were delighted with the result: a random pattern of vines and leaves safely crisscrosses the fountain jets, water lilies, and goldfish.

The choice of a predominately white garden was influenced by Mr. Lee's observation that white blossoms reflect light beautifully at night. Lighting was carefully chosen for this intimate space, with each tea olive softly lit to suggest candlelight. Mr. Lee felt that too much variety in a small space could spoil a formal effect. Reliance was placed on a small number of background plants, with potted plantings used for seasonal displays of color. Pairs of topiary ligustrums are used at the street and inner entrances.

Knowing the limitations of a garden, especially a small one, is important. The Lees avoided ambitious attempts at planting for summer bloom—it's too hot and humid, and the courtyard gets practically full sun. Pruning tasks continue year-round; the boxwood hedges are trimmed at least five times a year, and the topiaries and ivy swags require constant attention. "A good gardener is a good pruner," remarks Mr. Lee. "The size of the garden doesn't matter as much as what you do with it."

The Old Brewton Inn is now owned by designer Susan Cain Chick.

11

An Atrium Garden

When Dr. and Mrs. Morey Lipton were house-hunting two decades ago, they immediately realized the potential of a twenty-by-twenty foot atrium set in the middle of a contemporary house. Many other factors entered into their choice, but the courtyard was an exciting feature.

The Liptons knew they wanted the atrium to have the look and feel of a traditional Charleston garden. They considered using a landscape architect, and decided to consult Robert Marvin of Walterboro, South Carolina, who was working on several large projects in Charleston at the time.

Marvin's plan for the exterior had the contemporary feel of the house. Twelve river birches (*Betula nigra*) underplanted with Indian hawthorne (*Raphiolepis indica*) form a tall L-shaped hedge on the corner of the lot and continue behind the house. Low maintenance was an important request of the owners, and wide plantings of juniper against the house have proven to be a wise choice. The house sits near the marsh, and both the hawthorne and juniper are tolerant of salt spray. A wooden fence surrounds the rear of the property enclosing a patio and traditionally planted shrub and flower beds.

A delightful bonus has been the permission of friends to use an adjacent vacant lot for a large vegetable garden "sharecropped" by Dr. Lipton. Row upon row of Silver Queen corn, several varieties of tomatoes, eggplants, Vidalia onions, watermelons, beans, two or three squashes, beets, lots of peppers, cucumbers and potatoes flourish.

"This is an organic garden," says Dr. Lipton. "I use compost, organic fertilizer, and natural pesticides. Some crops, such as radishes left to go to seed, actually repel bugs. Permeable plastic mulch keeps the soil moist and warm. I use two types of tillers: a Troy-built pony and a twenty-pound Mantis. A portable cold frame comes in handy."

Winter crops vary, but usually include broccoli, cauliflower, Bok Choy and chinese cabbages and, of course, the delectable sugar snap peas.

While the vegetable garden needs daily attention when the crops come in, the atrium garden was planned for ease of care. Two of its surrounding glass panels are fixed; the north and west ones have sliding doors leading onto a short flight of old brick steps which cut through the raised beds onto a brick floor. These beds form a circle within the square, punctuated by an off-center low circle containing a holly tree and neatly clipped large-leaved Algerian ivy.

In three corners, the gnarled, sculptural trunks of heavily-pruned photina reach for the light, their leaves forming a soft canopy at roof-level. In the summer, shade-loving plants thrive beneath them, and Fatsia, aspidistra, nandina, and holly fern lend a variety of textures. Color is largely introduced using gay mixtures of impatiens, begonias, and caladiums. A handsome wrought iron table and chairs painted dark green are inviting; a bench and the wide brick edges of raised beds provide additional seating.

"Our atrium gives pleasure from every room of the house year-round," says Mrs. Lipton, "but I particularly enjoy taking my coffee and paper there in the morning. It's fun and very pretty for entertaining, too, especially when dramatically lit at night. For us, it has been the perfect Charleston garden."

Top right: This atrium garden, designed by landscape architect, Robert Marvin, extends only twenty-by-twenty feet. The edges of the raised brick borders are wide enough to provide seating. Mature multi-trunked photinias reach up from the corners of the garden. Other plants include fatsia, holly, and nandina. *Bottom right:* One of two sliding glass entrances into the atrium. Numerous potted plants allow for seasonal change and colorful accents.

Although the house was built on a large lot in 1765 and had always been a single family dwelling, no evidence of an early formal garden could be found when we purchased the property in 1982. Two brick outbuildings with tile roofs had been torn down in the 1930's or -40's, and the L-shaped yard had recently been subdivided.

We sought the advice of Mrs. Henry J. Lee, a local landscape designer, for a planting plan which would complement the house and give privacy from neighbors and a nearby school. We were almost ready to start placing trees and shrubs when we had the opportunity to purchase the subdivided lot and restore the property to its former size. This caused great excitement and began a wonderful family venture into landscape design and gardening.

My husband was highly enthusiastic and not only did quite a bit of research on plant material, but began to draw up designs for parterres and structures, based on Mrs. Lee's recommendations. He came up with a trellis suggestive of an interior fanlight, to be placed behind a slate terrace at the end of triple parterres, extending down the main axis of the house and garden. We moved hoses around for days trying to define borders and spent hours consulting gardening books. It wasn't long before we discovered the remains of a courtyard in hundreds of old bricks about a foot under the lawn, and dug them for the borders, along with more bricks from a path that led nowhere. We also dug up large areas of deep-rooted palmettos and a small street of buried cobblestones. Professionals removed a diseased elm, an equally dis-

A view of the garden from the house shows curving borders and formal parterres.

Top right: The house and garden from its western boundary. A pair of fig trees are espaliered against the porch and above an informal herb bed. *Bottom right:* A corner of a parterre, showing its border of Japanese holly, *Ilex crenata* 'Helleri.'

15

Caladiums line the entrance to the secret garden, which has an oriental theme.

eased hackberry, a crowded oak, and pruned the remaining trees. We were fortunate to have a stunning pair of Savannah hollies at the end of the garden, balanced on either side by an enormous magnolia and a willow oak.

For Valentine's Day, my husband gave me thirty rosebushes, which Mrs. Frank Heinsohn, a consulting rosarian, helped us choose for the parterres. Mrs. Lee pointed out the importance of anchoring the centers of the rosebeds, so we chose dwarf hollies (*Ilex crenata* 'Compacta') in the center of the rectangular beds and *Ilex crenata* 'Helleri' around the edges. It is a struggle to keep them neat and tidy, but their bluish-green foliage is worth the effort, and the beds are handsome year-round.

We took Mrs. Lee's advice to screen off a portion of the lot and make a surprise, or "secret" garden room, less formal than the main garden, reached by a winding, shaded path near the trellis. Nellie Stevens and Burford hollies were planted, along with five Leyland cypresses. The cypresses were remarkably fast growers, but unfortunately, the advantages of some plants become limitations in the long run. We

have found them to be shallow rooted and apt to blow over in a strong wind. They also take up a great deal of space. But they now camouflage our neighbor's bright green clapboards and are a lovely backdrop for a maple. Long-range plans for this area include an oriental garden as well as a shade garden.

A southern exposure along our northern boundary wall affords us the luxury of a sunny bed for annuals, perennials, and bulbs. Each year the challenge to coordinate and maintain bloom is renewed. So far, blue *salvias*, orange lantana, iris, chrysanthemums, and a collection of cannas and ginger lilies top the list for high perennial performance. Mary Zahl, a talented garden designer, recently helped us choose a variety of new plants to try in several areas. Poppies, lisianthus, and foxgloves are among our numerous failures. We are testing coreopsis, several types of daisies, rudbeckia 'Goldsturm,' and an unnamed goldenrod at the back of the herb bed near the house. Some of our best annuals are larkspur, which comes back from seed; pansies, which grow well here until June; stock, vinca, snapdragons, and impatiens, which we use with abandon. Hostas have done sur-

16

Purple and white stems of hosta reach through impatiens in a semi-shaded bed.

17

prisingly well in a shady border in front of reliable and showy azaleas. Favorite shrubs include gardenias, aucuba, fatsia, euonymous, hydrangeas, and tea olive. We have a great deal of wall space to cover and rely on jasmines, fig vine (*Ficus pumila*), clematis, and Carolina jessamine. We are hopeful that a variety of newly planted old-fashioned climbing roses will be an exciting addition. Flowering fruit trees and crape myrtles spaced at intervals lend verticality and bright color in the spring and fall above the beds of azaleas in the formal garden.

We work well as a team. I thoroughly enjoy pruning, weeding, and neatening, while my husband would rather move shrubs around or put in new plants. He is the diligent one when it comes to spraying, watering, mowing, and turning the compost heap, while I can spend days working out bulb orders and planting arrangements. Visiting nurseries and other gardens are favorite pastimes, but our greatest pleasures are sharing the garden with friends and enjoying the fruits of our labors. Coffee cup or glass in hand, we'll take a tour of our efforts, stopping to admire a successful arrangement or to discuss problem areas. In summer, from our screened porch, we watch the swifts swirl down the chimneys, followed by circling bats. We face west, and our sunsets can be spectacular.

Having recovered from summer's humidity and heat, the garden is usually at its peak in the fall. Chrysanthemums make a glorious show in the perennial bed with other hardy survivors of summer neglect, and the roses bloom profusely. Later, the cherry trees turn golden, the cut-leaf maple becomes lacquer-red, and the crape myrtles are green, gold and red, all at once. The fall weather is predictably mild, and we get a great deal accomplished. Bulbs go in around Christmas, trees in January, and the roses are pruned in February.

I love the look of the garden in winter. The evergreen shrubs and groundcovers are a handsome contrast to the neat hay-colored lawn, and there's something satisfactory and promising about the fresh, raked earth in the dormant perennial beds. In March, we make a tremendous effort to primp for the garden tours, but it's never quite as lovely as in June or October, when the garden is so lush we feel almost isolated from the busy city around us. We have seen

Above: In November, the perennial border is filled with purple spikes of salvia, orange lantana and chrysanthemums, white pentas, and silver dusty miller. *Top right:* Crape myrtles, morning glories and Kwanzan cherries provide a colorful fall display. *Bottom right:* Purple salvia, silver artemisia and dusty miller, orange lantana and zinnias bloom in the fall border.

hawks land on our lawn with their prey and once found a woodcock in the aspidistras.

In spite of our mild climate, we have suffered several major setbacks in the seven short years we've gardened, from unusually severe winters, to serious drought and a major hurricane. But we've always recovered and have looked forward to replanting, hoping it will be an opportunity to make changes for the better.

A Contemporary Courtyard

This early residence was built in 1740 by John Holmes, who later gave a one-block alley between Meeting and Church Streets to the city. The three-story stucco house now belongs to the Reverend Doctor and Mrs. William P. Rhett, who acquired it as rental property in 1971. Nine years later, they started on extensive renovations before making it their permanent home.

The only potential space for gardening was an eleven by twenty-three foot strip behind the house, completely enclosed by the residence, a neighboring three-story building, and a wall to the north. The area contained an outhouse which was removed; bricks from its demolition were used to heighten the common north wall, ensuring privacy.

Inspired by travels to Mykonos, Greece, and Palm Beach, Florida, the Rhetts decided to use evergreen topiary and vivid flowers in contrast with bright white walls, incorporating the color scheme of the spacious entrance hall with its white walls and colorful paintings. Two windows on either side of a French door leading from the hall into the garden were lowered to the floor to allow a better view.

In addition to three white walls, white cement and pebbles pave the courtyard floor, reflecting as much light as possible and creating an illusion of space. Off-white bricks were used for the raised planters and fish pond which extend in an irregular, fluid pattern along the wall facing the house. The street entrance is secured by a decorative wrought iron gate designed by the Rhetts. In the center of the gate is a gilded Great Egret, drawn to scale. A traditional lattice design forms the lower portion. At the top is a replica of a Celtic cross given to Doctor Rhett by a monastery.

Plant material was carefully chosen for year-round interest and shade tolerance. Three ligustrum trees, each trained in a different topiary form, accent the walls and corners. In winter, strips of brown paper wrapped around exposed branches protect the bark from cold damage. Boxwoods are pruned in rectangular shapes to contrast with the cone shapes of standard George Tabor azaleas. English ivy intertwined with a white clematis and a lavender wisteria arch over a bright pink camellia 'Jordans Pride.'

In late spring, after all danger of frost, bright lipstick pink impatiens and other shade-loving annuals are planted in the courtyard and in the elevated stucco trough near the gate. Pots of geraniums provide additional color. In the pool, goldfish slash among the pink and white water lilies and purple water hyacinths. A spiral juniper in a pale terra cotta single planter lends verticality and carries the eye up toward a pair of lion sculptures gazing down from the top of the wall.

Without crowding their small space, and working with limited sunlight, the Rhetts have arranged a successful combination of plant and structural materials, emphasizing a variety of forms as well as textures. Color is used primarily as an accent, but it also helps soften the edges of this courtyard which functions beautifully in its dual role as a garden and as an often-used extension of the house.

Right: Pink, green and white were chosen for the color scheme of this striking courtyard designed by the owners. In the far corner, a ligustrum has been painstakingly pruned into a form of Japanese topiary known as *tamazukuri.*

The Garden of the Thomas Rose House

When her husband purchased the Thomas Rose House in 1941, Mrs. Henry P. Staats had only seen the exterior and the small, sunny site beyond the porches which would be the start of her now much-acclaimed garden.

Interested from early childhood in observing and studying gardens, Mrs. Staats began gardening in earnest as a young bride living in the Connecticut countryside. On her first wedding anniversary, her mother-in-law presented her with an eighteenth-century bronze astrolabe, which she moved to subsequent gardens, and finally to Charleston.

"It was the focal point of the original garden space, and I designed an eighteenth-century brickwork pattern to surround it. I had loads of gardening books by this time, full of information on restoration and design."

But this was merely the beginning of an exciting venture into city gardening. A dilapidated house sat on the lot next door, which had originally been part of the lot attached to the Thomas Rose House. In the early 1950's it became available for sale.

"I had been lying in wait for years," recalled Mrs. Staats. "There was no question of restoring the house, and in 1954 we pulled it down, engaged Loutrel Briggs as our landscape architect, and installed the present garden."

The basic plan was for several areas: the parterre garden and lawn space in front of the kitchen buildings and a three-bay garage behind the house; a flagstone terrace; an oval lawn beyond the terrace with open-work brick walls and wrought iron gates leading to a kitchen garden; and a parking circle.

"I wanted open space, not enclosed, as well as a

Facing west, a large dogwood in full bloom marks the arrival of spring. Beyond the formal garden is a play area and greenhouse, hidden by shrubs and open-work brick walls.

An eastern view of the house, past a small terrace used for outdoor dining.

salad garden in the back with lots of herbs and a cutting garden, but I also wanted a mature garden as quickly as possible," she recounted.

Topsoil from Johns Island potato fields, well-rotted manure and truckloads of peat moss were delivered. Along with other shrubs, banks of azaleas, sasanquas, and camellias were planted and live oaks were carefully placed to shade the parking area and to camouflage neighboring buildings. A camellia collection divided the boundary of the rejoined lot with entrances to the terrace and across the long lawn to the kitchen garden. The camellias, which today tower as high as twelve to fifteen feet, are largely old-fashioned varieties, including 'Hermes' variegated, the red 'C.D. Sargent,' formal white 'Imura,' the much loved 'Pink Perfection,' and the 'Lady Vansittart' variegated, which sports red, pink and variegated blooms on an individual bush.

Other specimens for the new garden proved a challenge to find. A Lusterleaf holly (*Ilex latifolia*) was discovered upstate in an abandoned area and successfully transplanted. Mrs. Staats' patience was rewarded when, after a two-year wait, a local nurseryman dug a particularly fine sweet bay from a nearby swamp. Gordonia, a heavy summer bloomer and native to South Carolina, was finally located, but numerous attempts to establish it were unsuccessful until botanical literature revealed that the plants wanted morning light and "not a ray of afternoon sun."

Sculpture was also to become an integral part of the garden. In 1978, Mrs. Staats commissioned the American sculptor, Henry Mitchell, whose work was contemporary, yet traditional in style, to make bronze figures for placement at either side of the terrace. These were designed in two pairs, intended to represent the four seasons, with Spring and Summer standing, and Fall and Winter kneeling. The standing figures hold baskets (a popular eighteenth-century motif) which can be filled with arranged or potted plants.

Mr. Mitchell, who knew the garden well, made the trip from his Swiss home, via his foundry in Milan,

23

Top: An armillary sphere is featured in the pattern garden, where a low yew hedge surrounds dwarf azaleas. At the edges are the strap-like leaves of scilla, which send up racemes of blue in late spring. *Bottom:* One of two bronze figure pairs designed for the garden, surrounded by several specimens of the owner's camellia collection.

Recently replanted, the borders of the formal lawn contain vividly colored azaleas in contrast with pale pink raphiolepsis and bright limemound spirea.

25

to oversee the installation. Sadly, he died very shortly after his arrival in 1980. A pair of bronze prancing unicorns were a gift from his widow. Terra-cotta squirrels by Willard Hirsch, a well-known Charleston sculptor, chatter at each other across a gate to the service area.

The garden matured beautifully, but gardens, like houses, need to be renovated and restored. In 1988, a few years after two successive devastating winters and the loss of numerous plants (including two large *Magnolia x soulangianas*), Hugh Dargan Associates was brought in to revitalize the garden and solve some major problems. The oaks, although meticulously pruned each year, had covered a large part of the garden in shade, so new plantings included aucuba species, new varieties of azaleas, several yews, numerous leatherleaf ferns, *Fatsia japonica*, the tea plant (*Camellia sinensis*), variegated gardenias, cley-

Carolina jessamine, the state flower, blooms above the wrought iron gates of the kitchen garden, now a play area.

Terracotta squirrels chatter at each other from the gateposts to a service area. Lavender wisteria vine softens the edge of the garage, casting a graceful shadow across its facade.

era, limemound spirea, pittosporum, and two types of viburnums. Many established plants were shifted, a new semi-circular bed was created near the rear entrance to the house, and the demands of young family members now in residence were considered with the creation of a play area in the former kitchen garden. A greenhouse had been tucked into this space for some time after its initial planning, and it was refurbished for its new tenants, including favorite orchids and a spectacular pair of yellow camellias. Placed in pots and featured on the terrace, the camellias are carefully moved to avoid sun and often have to be netted to keep squirrels from savoring the sweet, waxy buds.

Thus lovingly tended, the garden flourishes, and, designed with a showy spring bloom and entertaining in mind, it is frequently the scene of *al fresco* luncheons and elegant suppers. Mrs. Staats sums up her successions of seasons in the garden with the remark, "One of my greatest pleasures is that I have lived long enough to see my garden come to maturity, and that is fortunate indeed."

A Charleston-made joggling board furnishes the porch, opening onto a view of the garden in early spring.

A Small Colorful Garden

Although neither the house nor the small garden is old, both are surrounded by the venerable brick walls and facades of the historic district and stand in the southern portion of what used to be the service yard and dependencies of a nineteenth-century Church Street dwelling.

After removal of a garage, the garden was created twelve years ago by the present owners with the help of Robert Chestnut, a local landscape architect. In keeping with its surroundings, brick was used for the paving and walls, and plant material was carefully chosen to achieve the look and feel of openness.

Spacious beds surround a neat square of lawn which is kept immaculately clipped, as is the fig vine covering the east and west walls. Only two trees were planted: a Kwanzan cherry for spring flowering, and a white crape myrtle for summer bloom.

Color is evident nearly year-round due to the owners' practice of setting blooming nursery plants in the well-prepared beds at least three times a year. "I was brought up in New York City," explains Beverly Colman. "My single gardening experience was the pur-

An unusual candelabra provides a focal point, dramatic contrast, and soft lighting for the terrace.

Begonias and impatiens bloom in early summer beneath a crape myrtle and a Kwanzan cherry in this small garden designed by landscape architect Robert Chesnut.

28

A colorful display of tulips and primroses, which require treatment as short-lived annuals in this climate.

chase of three tomato plants. They flourished, and I got so excited about them that I sent photographs to a friend in England, who promptly returned them with ink marks showing where the tomatoes should have been pruned!" Bedding plants offer the luxury of instant seasonal show and are a reasonable expenditure for such a small area.

The sunny beds hold a succession of tulips, daffodils, pansies, snapdragons, daisies, geraniums, begonias, impatiens, zinnias, and chrysanthemums. Pots of herbs used in cooking line the terrace and its steps. There are some lovely perennials, too, including phlox and a stunning hedge of yellow bush daisies along the front fence. "I grow several plants from seed and use a portable cold frame and take cuttings every fall. Some of my daisies are tenth and eleventh generation."

The family has spent many summers abroad, bringing back several wonderful garden ornaments, such as a lovely stone fountain from Florence, which was installed as the garden's focal point. An enor-

mous Cherokee rose that used to tumble gracefully from the building above the fountain was unfortunately amputated by a neighbor's roofers, but a replacement has been planted. The wrought iron gates of the property were copied from a pair of nineteenth-century Italian gates. A huge terra-cotta olive oil jar anchors a corner near the drive.

Miss Colman has had success with more than tomato plants as proven in the garden log she keeps, complete with clippings and photographs. A graduate of Clemson University's first Master Gardener program in Charleston, she devotes many volunteer hours to the local extension service, offering help and advice by telephone and at plant clinics. A serious gardener, but ever humorous, she has dubbed her well-trained dog the official "under-gardener." On pleasant days one may find them both contemplating their work from an old (but not Charleston-made) bench Miss Colman calls the "piazza," a witty reference to Charleston's stately porches.

Rosemary Verey, in her book, *The Garden in Winter*, points out the importance of creating pleasant views of the garden from the principal rooms of a house. Mr. and Mrs. Blaine Ewing, owners of this delightful "pocket" garden, had just such ideas in mind when they were implementing their design.

The property consisted of two lots when purchased; the portion allotted for garden space was, in fact, a yard with some lawn, no formal flower beds, ivy everywhere, and assorted overgrown shrubs. Enthusiastic in-laws who were experienced gardeners suggested using the perspective from the second floor porch as a point of reference for laying out the lawn and beds. Many designs were outlined using garden hoses. The final result is most pleasant indeed.

A utility area for cars and boats was effectively screened by using small trees and lattice. Dogwoods were a good choice, as they lend verticality with an open pattern and have the added attraction of bloom. Wisteria, which usually blooms with the dogwoods, cascades down the walls along the street. In the planning, the Ewings felt they needed a focal point as one entered the street gate entrance. They found a wall fountain which met space limitations and made a raised lily pond against the far garden wall. A brick terrace in front of the pond provides an area for outdoor dining and entertaining.

Plantings were considered particularly for color and fragrance. Tea olive (*Osmanthus frangrans*), the dominant tree next to the house, blooms several

One of several paths from the lawn, this one leads toward a raised brick pond covered with a white Lady Banks rose.

A white Lady Banks rose covers a small fishpond with an edge wide enough for seated contemplation.

times a year. Banana shrub (*Michelia Figo*), another favorite in the Charleston garden, is also planted near the house and sports pale yellow flowers that not only smell like bananas, but subtly resemble them. *Daphne odora*, while difficult to grow, is rewarding for its intense, heady fragrance. Very sweet and spectacular is the Chinese wisteria, which requires disciplined pruning to keep it within bounds.

"We've tried to stay with plant material that's native, having wasted much time, effort and expense on tempting exotics that failed to thrive, and had diseases and pest problems," notes Mr. Ewing. "Four or five years after creating the garden, however, we decided to put in a greenhouse. Orchids and other indoor plants were overflowing a third floor bedroom, and we needed to winter over some favorite exotics such as jatropha, which has glossy dark green foliage and stunning red flowers."

Color predominates from March through late May. Yellow, pink and white are favorite combinations. The Ewings ascribe to the theory that a garden should be roughly fifty percent white. In accordance, perennial candytuft, a succession of daisies, including May Queen and Alaska varieties, ginger lilies (*Hedychium coronarium*), amaryllis, 'G. G. Gerbing' azaleas, the showy double 'Snow' azaleas, gardenias, baby's breath, spirea, Confederate jasmine, and dogwoods provide the desired effect. Snapdragons are long-lasting annuals best planted in fall, which give excellent choices in the warmer color range. Scilla, larkspur, and iris provide cool touches of blue. Red and orange are used as accents, such as the orange epidendrum orchids hung in the low trees, containers of red geraniums, and spots of crimson impatiens.

"So far we haven't planted specifically for summer bloom," says Mr. Ewing, "as we don't enjoy a labor-intensive garden in the hot summer months. But daylilies, vinca, and portulaca tolerate the heat well. Winter interest is important—we like to see the structure of the garden. Iris lends wonderful texture; nandina and hollies are showy; camellias are peaceful; 'R. L. Wheeler' is a favorite. The pink flowering apricot is a recent acquisition; we wanted something that would bloom in January."

31

Scale and proportion are important. Although hardy and colorful, oleander was discarded because it grew too large, too quickly. Size and growth habits aren't the only limitations. "We tried the exquisite pink native azalea with no success. There have been problems with soil alkalinity, but the bedding plants like it and mahonias flourish." The climbing 'Peace' and 'Joseph's Coat' roses have done well, as has the wild Cherokee rose, which can be seen in the Lowcountry in spring, spilling its single white blossoms over fences and climbing up into trees and shrubs.

"We are always eager to learn more about gardening and find taking notes when visiting gardens and nurseries is most helpful," continues Mr. Ewing. "Actually seeing new plant material gives a feel for what may work best when considering proportion, depth and texture, and that is what we enjoy the most about the garden we've created—it feels right for us."

Top: Spirea, dogwood and wisteria compete for attention in a spring burst of bloom. *Left:* A brilliant red branch of Oregon grape (*Mahonia*) highlights a shady area near the gate. *Right:* An arch supporting Carolina jessamine crosses over the path from the driveway.

32

An Historic Garden Restoration

The recent recipient of a prestigious merit award from the American Society of Landscape Architects, this garden was also featured in Penelope Hobhouse's book, *Color In Your Garden*, and has received much local and national attention. Owned by Mrs. Roger P. Hanahan, the garden is, in part, one of the few extant eighteenth-century gardens in the city. It was restored in 1983-1984 by Hugh Dargan Associates.

The L-shaped white clapboard house, which dominates a corner in the historic district, was finished by 1800. A two-story porch, incorporating the front entrance on its first level, overlooks the garden to the west.

From the street, a tall pair of wrought iron gates centered in aged brown brick walls open onto the old pattern garden. Paths of crushed oyster shells and sand surround the brick-bordered beds filled with old-fashioned annuals and perennials. The pattern, meant to be viewed from the house, is made up of four ovals placed around a central diamond. Similar patterns were often found in eighteenth-century European designs.

A second garden is entered through a wooden, groin-vaulted arbor flanked by specimen thirty-foot crape myrtles and ten-foot camellias, among other plantings. Largely hidden from the street, this garden is composed of a grass panel surrounded by beds of shrubbery and small trees. At one end is a fountain with a statue and pool; at the other is a slate terrace partially covered by a trellis-work roof.

Mrs. Hanahan purchased the property as a restoration project. The house was in poor condition, and the garden, once documented as well-kept, had the appearance of a vacant lot. Mrs. Hanahan contacted landscape architect Hugh Dargan, citing her need for skillful blending of house and grounds, historical authenticity, pretty views, privacy, and a place for outdoor entertaining. It was during Mr. Dargan's initial visit that the brick borders of the old pattern garden, dimly outlined in the grass and weeds, were revealed under a layer of earth.

Working with landscape architect Mary Palmer Dargan, a general contractor, a landscape contractor, an archeologist, a horticulturist, and an architectural preservation consultant, Hugh Dargan Associates put together a team of thirteen craftsmen. A brick wall was constructed at the north end of the lot to match the existing south street wall. To give it a look of age and encourage the growth of moss and mold, a sludge of oyster shells, yeast, motor oil, plaster, and cow manure was applied.

Plant material of species and varieties dating from the late 1700's was painstakingly researched and is the highlight of the garden. To give the garden an immediate, established look, the largest possible specimens were located and strategically placed. Part of the garden's appeal is that there is an interesting focal point or view from every angle. Opposite the porches, to the west, a large stone urn from England is centered in front of three palmettos. Through the arbor, beyond the "sitting" garden lawn, one glimpses an eighteenth-century sundial placed in an arch of the wall. Standard roses lend a vertical dimension to the parterres of the front garden.

Attention was given to the smallest details: French doors leading from the garage to the terrace hide automobile bumpers; garden lighting received special attention; cypress wood was used for the trellis over the terrace.

Through the pattern of ovals, diamonds, and arches in the wrought iron of the handsome old gates opening into the garden, the passerby can see not only a repeat of these designs in the beds, arbor, and walls, but also, in the words of Mary Palmer Dargan, "the owner's gift of a view into garden history."

Top: A water *putto* dances in the rear garden. Raphiolepis blooms in the foreground. *Bottom: Rose chinesis* 'Mutabilis,' the butterfly rose, is planted in the central parterre and repeated on the wooden groin-vaulted arbor leading to the back garden.

35

A Classical Garden

During construction of the city's municipal auditorium just north of the historic Ansonborough district, a large circa 1799 house was conveyed to the Historic Charleston Foundation and moved one-hundred feet to its present location. A sympathetic brick extension was added, and the two-story porches, which had been enclosed, were torn off and replaced with Doric columns and balusters from another restoration. The grocery store on the lot was demolished, making room for a garden in front, and a pair each of magnolias and hollies were the initial plantings within the new brick boundaries.

When the property was purchased by Mr. and Mrs. Chet Kellogg in 1973, they did not plan to move to Charleston for several years. The contract with the Historic Charleston Foundation, however, stipulated that a garden had to be laid out within a year of sale, so the family got to work.

Designed entirely by the Kelloggs, the formality of this garden anticipates and complements the formality of the house and its interior.

A pedestrian gate opens into an airy court of lawn facing the house, enclosed by low open-work brick walls draped with Confederate jasmine. Initially, gravel paths were laid out in the pattern of a cross with a central circular fountain for a focal point, but the gravel was soon replaced by brick, which required much less maintenance.

The owners wanted to achieve the look and feel of an eighteenth-century Charleston garden, using modern plant material and their own design. Low boxwoods and four topiary photinia surround a black urn fountain; six handsome palmettos effectively punctuate the lawn and define the fountain garden as a separate area.

The eye is drawn to the imposing brick stairs guarded by a stunning pair of black dogs made in New York in 1850, up the porches to the entrance. Keeping low maintenance a top priority, the beds in front of the house are planted with shrub roses, azaleas, and crinum lilies.

Gates for the driveway are located near the pedestrian gate, and the drive is incorporated into the garden through use of the same brick paving, complementary plantings, and widening a section to give the effect of a terrace. A replica of an eighteenth-century Italian cherub smiles from the center of alternating ligustrum and pittosporum hedges, flanked by a pair of carefully pruned white rose of Sharon (*Hibiscus syriacus*) specimens.

Design, symmetry, and texture play the important roles in what is largely a shrubbery garden. Unsightly neighboring buildings to the east presented a challenge met by repetitious plantings of hardy photinia and loquats. The loquat, or Japanese plum, is an excellent small evergreen tree for specimen plantings, screens, or espaliers. The common variety has glossy deep-green leaves with a coarse texture accented by pale new growth, and bears clusters of soft creamy flowers. It produces edible yellow-orange fruit surrounding a large seed, which is highly prized by local children not only for its sweetness, but also for the seed's projectile qualities.

A third, more private section lies off the kitchen addition, past raised beds for annuals. One small bed is outlined in the shape of the legs of a curule chair, a reflection of the owners' interest in period furnishings and garden ornaments. The whole area has just recently been planted and is enhanced by soft pink stucco walls. Several wrought iron fern pattern benches made in Philadelphia around 1870 provide seating in the shade; a touch of fancy is added by a large French sphinx whose face is that of Madame DuBarry.

Once anxious for the garden to take on an established look as quickly as possible, the owners now cite keeping the luxuriant growth of their hardy plantings under control as a major, but enjoyable task.

Top: The cylindrical pruning of photinias around the fountain is repeated on hollies at the entrance to the house. Old-fashioned crinum lilies bloom by the steps. *Bottom:* Palmettos cast late afternoon shadows across the front lawn.

Top left: A view of the front lawn from the second story porch. Pink crape myrtles are just coming into bloom. *Bottom:* Elephant's ears and impatiens in a shaded court. *Above:* Madame DuBarry keeps watch over a small paved court planted with hydrangeas and canna lilies.

The framed photograph hanging near a window overlooking the garden shows a surprising view of the house in the 1850's from across a tidal basin. Eventually, like much of the marsh on the southern and western edges of the peninsula, the land was filled for homesites.

Twelve years ago, Mr. and Mrs. T. Hunter McEaddy purchased and began restoration of the house. There was little, if any, evidence of a garden in the barren space beyond the porches, which face south. A coal house and an unsightly garage were removed, and a landscape architect drew plans.

These plans, however, were never implemented. Coming from a family of architects and gardeners, Hunter McEaddy decided to combine his inherited talents and began a graduate program in landscape architecture, commuting to the nearest school, which was in Georgia. Six years later, he began construction of his own garden.

Explaining the basic rectilinear layout, Mr. McEaddy acknowledges an instinctive approach mixed, in this case, with the very practical need for a play area for his five children and a sentimental desire for the garden paths he remembered running along in his grandmother's garden.

The plan is a rectangular lawn within a larger rectangle of bordering flower beds surrounded by stone pathways. To the west, effectively screened by evergreen shrubs and a fifty-seven-year-old magnolia, lies a much narrower rectangle containing a generous play yard and playhouse/storage shed. Utility areas, cutting, and experimental flower beds are on the opposite side of the lawn, partially screened by ornamental trees. To the south, beyond the lawn, is a small shady terrace with a reflecting pool in front of an open, wooden pergola. This "summerhouse" purposely reflects the form of the old house opposite.

Pennsylvania blue stone was chosen for the paths for several reasons, including color, harmony, and repetition of a rectilinear theme. In addition, the McEaddys were interested in achieving the effect of an English country garden, especially one with a little Victorian exuberance.

At its peak in summer, the garden is as profusely exuberant as hoped. Scotch roses spill across the stones to meet oleander boughs heavy with an abundance of pink blossoms; cannas and marigolds mix happily, and the shrub roses in the perennial border are in full bloom. The roses were selected for their ever-blooming characteristics, scent, and low form; hybrid teas were ruled out. Some of the choices were 'Champneys' Pink Cluster,' 'Louis Philippe,' 'Caldwell Pink,' 'Salet,' and 'Cartier.' The polyantha 'China Doll' and the floribunda 'Betty Prior' are also included.

Within the borders, handsome boxwoods accent corners and path entrances; dogwoods and crape myrtles provide a sculptural touch; giant liriope is an unusual accent; and tropicals are encouraged in a wilder corner near the reflecting pond. The pond, only a few inches deep, has been filled just once and requires little care, but satisfies the urge to grow a few aquatic plants. The goldfish are all prizes from children's carnivals. Pots of impatiens help brighten the shady area around the terrace and pool and are also used beneath trees near the entrance to the house. Azaleas and camellias, used sparingly in the main garden, line the drive.

Surveying his creation, Hunter McEaddy candidly remarks, "Of all the designs I've done, I like my garden the best, and it gives me great pleasure that my work is also my hobby."

Right: A view from the cutting garden. Nandina shows its white flowers and red berries on the left.

A Palm Collector's Garden

A recent visitor to this garden remarked, "Why, this is more like being in the Bahamas than in Charleston." This comment was elicited by the profusion of palms and other tropical specimens casually arranged in a series of paisley-like island beds which fill the generous space behind the house. Various paths intersect each other; benches invite contemplation of select groupings of plants; statuary abounds. Tucked behind an extension of the house are a small kitchen garden and a greenhouse. A roughly-paved path alongside the vegetables leads to a pool and open lawn, edged with a few large palms and many immature ones of large varieties.

An active member of the International Palm Society, Dr. George DelPorto grew his first palm many years ago from a date seed. "I like the primitive, exotic quality of palms," he explains. "I have also always enjoyed visiting the tropics and was interested in tropical plants."

From a greenhouse in Tennessee, where he and his wife lived during medical residency, an increasing palm collection was brought to Charleston and expanded to the outdoor garden.

Some palms came from seed collections offered through mail-order catalogs, others were ordered through a seed bank advertised in the Palm Society's scientific journal, *Principes*, and many were dug from the gardens of other palm enthusiasts. Once established, palms are relatively disease- and pest-free. Cold damage can present a serious problem, but a number of palms are hardy in our climate.

Patience and careful planning are keys to successful palm growing, as many of them take five to ten years to develop the beautiful trunks which are so desirable. Certain species also grow to tremendous size and therefore need to be chosen and located accordingly. Thorns or spikes on trunks and leaves can be hazardous, like those of the Acrocomia species, also known as Gru-Gru palms. One such specimen in the DelPorto garden, found through a collector in Deland, Florida, is rarely available at nurseries because of its vicious spikes.

The rarest palm in Dr. DelPorto's collection is one also purchased from another collector, an F2 hybrid of *Butia capitata* (the jelly palm) and *Jubaea spectabilis* (a honey palm from Chile). Included also are the windmill or hemp palm (*Trachycarpus Fortunei*), the Chinese fan palm (*Livistona chinensis*), the Canary Islands date palm (*Phoenix canariensis*), the Puerto Rican hat palm (*Sabal causiarum*), the needle or porcupine palm (*Rhapidophyllum hystrix*) which is native to South Carolina, and of course, the Sabal palmetto, our state tree. Deep green cycads, which are related to and frequently mistaken for palms, sport deep yellow and orange blossoms near Christmas. Two date palms (*Phoenix dactylifera*) from California are growing well, but prefer a less humid climate. "I think palms are prettiest when grown closely together, the way they occur naturally," remarks Dr. DelPorto. "Space is my limiting factor."

The tropical atmosphere created by the palms is enhanced by a large stand of bamboo and a row of banana trees which bear fruit. Also productive are a lemon tree and a satsuma orange with at least a dozen fruits. A vegetable patch provides less exotic home-grown edibles.

Certain dwarf palms and understory palms are planted in shady areas along with the typical azaleas, sasanquas, and camellias of a Charleston garden. A pair of *Cunninghamia* (China fir) specimens are doing well, and oleander thrives.

The garden also includes an olive tree, which is usually strictly ornamental in our climate. Papyrus combines successfully with the fronds of smaller palms, and there is a hardy version of the bamboo palm so often seen as a houseplant.

Like all collectors, Dr. DelPorto is always searching for the unusual. "We saw a mature *Butia capitata* 'strictior' at Disney World, and I'd love to find a plant for sale. It won't come true from seed." This variety has leaves "like an ostrich plume" and would be a lovely addition to the already tremendous variety of texture and color found in this unusual Charleston garden.

Heavy fruit of the South American jelly palm (*Butia capitata*), one of the hardiest of exotic palms.

43

Palms and pittosporum at the driveway entrance to the garden.

Top: One of many statues in this eclectic garden of a palm collector. *Bottom left:* Early morning sunlight is broken into a kaleidoscopic pattern by palm trees along the drive. In the background, a large white oleander is in full summer bloom. *Bottom right:* Bright red azaleas provide a striking contrast with palm fronds and rye grass.

45

Stewardship and gardening sometimes go hand in hand. In the 1940's the Kittredge family, creators of the famous Cypress Gardens near Charleston, lived in one of the oldest houses in the city and created a garden around it with the help of Umberto Innocenti, a well-known American landscape architect. The energetic and imaginative steward of this garden is now Mrs. Andrew Drury, who bought the property several years ago.

There are seven distinct garden "rooms," each separated by low walls, gates, or shoulder-height hedges of shrubbery. Fanciful iron work is a hallmark of the garden, and there is a view from every direction. An entrance walkway lined with azaleas branches off near a carriage house with its own ivy court and a separate lawn surrounded by raised beds. In the other direction, there are two paved rectangular courts hedged with holly, a raised statuary garden, a formal parterre garden, and an oak grove. A stone-marked pet graveyard has a special spot.

The formal garden of azalea-filled boxwood parterres features small statues of the four seasons and an armillary sundial. Conical and spherical topiaries echo statuary shapes along a scalloped, terra-cotta colored stucco wall. The topiary theme is playfully carried out with the addition of several life-size deer forms covered with fig vine. According to some, the Kittredges discovered the paving and outlines of this formal area under several inches of dirt.

One of the most stunning views is from the western porch looking north. Beyond a paved court and under spreading live oak limbs, steps lead up to a small terrace with a large statue of a crane in flight. California variegated privet and dwarf bamboo provide a green background, while the stained glass windows of a neighboring church loom high up in its brick facade at the end of the property.

"There used to be lawns instead of these mossy courts," explains Mrs. Drury, "but shade, dogs, and dampness led to paving. I put the crane there soon after we moved here as a focal point." Now she daily feeds a flock of birds on the bricks in front.

"I love a formal garden," continues Mrs. Drury. "I want my garden neat, defined, and symmetrical in all but a few areas." In the grove garden, for instance, where nine straight oak trunks punctuate the lawn, the border beds are irregular and the feeling is almost woods-like, as opposed to formal. Most plants tend to be in groups, in pairs, and well-trimmed. "Some gardeners say you should always have blue in the garden, but I really prefer purple," she remarks. 'George Tabor' azaleas are a favorite in the lavender shades, and wisteria is trained along the front of the carriage house. Pear trees are featured in a couple of areas, and topiary forms are seen in pots or framing an entrance. A pair of rabbits pop up near a door; ivy cones define a small space.

Numerous areas have required much thought and care in the re-working. Mrs. Drury highly recommends Algerian ivy as a groundcover for problem areas. She has an excellent helper in landscape contractor Will Simmons, but admits, like many other gardeners, to be positively driven when it comes to the garden. "I'm constantly doing work that isn't absolutely necessary, and I find that there's always so very much more to do," she laughs.

Right: One of several paved courts. Algerian ivy provides a lush, effective ground cover.

46

A mossy path along a paved court leads to the porch. Yellow Carolina jessamine is kept in bounds on one of a series of decorative supports.

Top: the "bones" of the garden are clearly outlined in this view facing north. *Bottom:* The formal parterre and topiary garden in early spring.

A fine example of what many would call a "typical Charleston garden" lies behind the brick wall and ornate wrought iron gates of this elegant residence. Construction on the house began in 1764 and was completed by 1770. In 1781, Hessian officers were quartered there during the Revolutionary War, and it is reported that one of the first Christmas trees ever raised in the Western Hemisphere decorated the house during the Hessian occupation.

The lot, like so many in the old city, is long, narrow, and shaded. Mrs. G. Kirkwood King, who purchased the property in 1959, knew exactly the sort of garden she wished to create. In fact, she had previously owned a house across the street and had helped design its lovely entrance.

Her late husband had been an avid gardener, propagating many plants and always encouraging and emphasizing gardening. It was his camellias and azaleas that Mrs. King brought with her from Greenville in 1959 to plant in the new garden. Loutrel Briggs was consulted for his advice on a general design which would be effective when viewed from the triple porches of the house, and also for his suggestions on the placement of plants chosen by Mrs. King.

One can approach the garden from either the entrance porch or the driveway gates. An oval lawn surrounded with shade-loving evergreen camellias, sasanquas, azaleas, nandinas, and borders of holly ferns and liriope is dominated by an enormous live oak to the east, the house to the north, and a variety

Left: The Colonel Isaac Motte house, viewed from the garden. *Above:* A tall hedge of azaleas and camellias surrounds the east garden beneath an enormous live oak.

of trees to the south along the drive. The overscale size of the trees lends an air of enclosure and privacy so much in keeping with the feel of Charleston city gardens.

The lawn narrows at its eastern end and leads into another shrub-encircled garden beneath the huge oak. The central bed, filled with creeping jasmine, was designed by Mrs. King's son, Joseph Maybank. Only the oak, a single camellia, and the Lady Banks rose cascading over the edge of the porch were originally in the garden. Now, Burford hollies and ligustrum give height along the walls and in the back of the wide beds. A large peach tree and a dogwood contrast with the dark green of a huge cedar; a tall ginkgo tree provides brilliant yellow fall color. For difficult areas such as the parking space beyond the garden, bamboo is an effective screen, as are various hollies. Yaupon holly and eleagnus are shrubs which tolerate adverse growing conditions and can be easily shaped. Cast iron plant (*Aspidistra elatior*) makes a good filler for shady low spots, while variegated aucuba, with its green and yellow leaves, is useful for brightening and filling dark areas.

To complement the cool, deep tones of the garden, grey slag was chosen for the driveway surface. Paths are of brick or flagstone. The entrance porch, with its stone floor on the same level as the lawn, is a natural transition from the house to the garden. Pots of ferns, aspidistra, and geraniums are casually arranged around benches, creating an inviting vantage point for enjoying the well-balanced texture and arrangement of the garden beyond.

51

Top: The fresh white blossoms of a Lady Banks rose and a dogwood tree balance the hot pinks and reds of azaleas and camellias. *Bottom:* South view from a secluded path. *Right:* This paved entrance porch leads directly into the garden opposite and beyond the house.

Built as a winter home by Isaac Jenkins Mikell, a cotton planter, this majestic house was completed, along with its garden, in 1854. The house, built in the classic revival style with Greek and Italian features, has been called a notable example of "the only thoroughly American architecture." It is believed that at least a portion of the garden still retains its original design.

Each fall, the Mikell family traveled the forty miles from their Edisto Island plantation to be in Charleston for the winter, but after the Civil War, Mr. Mikell decided to give up the house due to "the distressing condition of the country in this section." It remained in private hands until 1935, when it was purchased as the new home for the Charleston County Library.

While the house was used as the library, the grounds were kept by the Garden Club of Charleston. A newspaper article of 1935 described the spacious garden as "filled with rare and lovely flowers of many varieties, plants of various kinds, especially choice bulbs, as well as the Sago palm, stately magnolias, camellias and palmettos, which are now said to be the finest in the city. The palmettos were brought to the home from Edisto Island."

The house and garden were both threatened by possible development in 1960, when the library moved to its present King Street location, but preser-

Left: A view overlooking the garden, where a swimming pool replaced one of the formal parterres. *Above:* The grand portico of the Jenkins-Mikell house.

vation efforts resulted in the sale of the property to Mr. and Mrs. Charles H. Woodward of Philadelphia and Charleston. The Woodwards were responsible for extensive restoration of the house and the grounds.

Today, the house continues to be enjoyed as a family residence. Recent owners have retained the formality of the garden, adding statuary and a pool in place of a parterre. Designed to be viewed from the house, the main garden presents itself as a pattern of ovals and circles surrounded by boxwood parterres. Soft red crushed brick lines the paths and provides year-round color and contrast. Plant material is also formal; boxwoods, azaleas, yew, Sago palms and hollies provide structure. Fatsia lends an exotic touch,

while Asian jasmine and Algerian ivy are effective groundcovers.

The most recent owners, Mr. and Mrs. Joseph Land, have continued the tradition of restoring and carefully maintaining the garden. In 1987, they consulted landscape architect Sheila Wertimer, and began the refurbishing and reworking constantly required in a garden. A handsome row of magnolias along the southern garden boundary had become diseased and was replaced with large specimens. Privacy hedges were replanted, but a small opening was graciously planned to allow a view from the sidewalk of this splendid Victorian garden.

"It reminded me of the book, *The Secret Garden*," smiled the owner, while recalling her first impression of the large property downtown. The distinguished house and garden had been on the market for over a year, and the garden was quickly being overcome by a riot of lush growth.

Built in the early 1770's, the house was occupied by several different families, including the Draytons, who were the founders of Magnolia Gardens near Charleston. Almost an acre of land lies totally enclosed by high brick walls beyond the imposing facade and handsome fence. Very few historical facts about the garden have surfaced, but one eighteenth-century reference alludes to numerous orange trees, which were then fashionable among wealthy Europeans. A charming open brick summerhouse contains an exact replica of the marble bas-relief on the Drayton family tomb at Magnolia Gardens, carved by the Italian sculptor, Jardella, who came to America in the 1790's.

In the 1930's, Mrs. Washington Roebling, whose husband built the Brooklyn Bridge, purchased the property and began extensive renovations and restoration. She was extremely interested in the garden, and employed Loutrel Briggs to draw up comprehensive formal plans, including some of the ironwork, ornaments, and architectural features.

Over fifty years later, faced with overgrown boxwood parterres, the remnants of a rose garden, crumbling brick and stone, and paved walkways in upheaval, Mr. and Mrs. W. Jefferson Leath consulted Hunter McEaddy, a local landscape architect.

Hydrangeas, oleander and lantana display summer color at the east gate. An evergreen pittosporum provides privacy.

Large crape myrtles are planted throughout the garden and put on a glorious summer show. The elegant brick folly in the background was designed to be roofless.

The lily pond in bloom. Hardy lilies bloom for several days in the summer, opening in the morning and closing in the afternoon. Liriope, which sends up purple spikes, surrounds the pool.

Urns filled with impatiens brighten the garden in July.

"We wanted the garden to retain its air of mystery, romance, and even disuse, but at the same time we hoped to create a contemporary rather than a reproduction garden," notes Mrs. Leath. From the front door of the house, a sixty-foot hall leads out onto a double staircase descending to the garden. An allée of brick pillars capped with stone extends down this central axis, and a swimming pool shimmers beyond in place of Mrs. Roebling's flagstone court. "We felt that the uneven flagstones looked amorphous; there was no focal point at the end of our vista. We also had planned on a garden the children could really use, so a pool was a clever solution," remarks Mrs. Leath.

Mr. McEaddy adds that it was a challenge to honor the existing garden design while offering a functional plan for the current owners' purposes. The pool presented the main design problem. An ornamental character was needed, so slate on the property was used for the surround, providing an irregular edge and an overhang that gives wonderful shadow lines. Lampblack was mixed with the concrete for a dark, mottled bottom.

The corners of the pool area were accented with four huge boxwoods transplanted from other loca-

tions in the garden. A pittosporum hedge was planted to give privacy from the nearby parking court. To the west, a greenhouse was torn down in the kitchen garden and a perennial bed established on the pool side. A huge bed of daylilies and another of hydrangeas provide abundant summer color.

During the project, much excitement occurred when a local antiques dealer called to announce that a copy of Mr. Briggs' long-lost plans for the garden had turned up. Among other discoveries, the drawings revealed parterres where there was lawn. A daughter's optimistic and enthusiastic digging unearthed the original brick borders beneath nearly a foot of soil.

Hundreds of boxwoods needed replacement, a new rose garden was installed, lawns were renewed, the graceful picket fence along the kitchen garden repaired, and a gardener was employed to help with the tremendous maintenance chores. "I pay the children to wade into the goldfish pond and fertilize the waterlilies; no one else wants to take on that job," says their mother. "Each child has an additional task in the garden—mine as a girl in Louisiana was to deadhead the gardenias and roses. I feel that the very best way to learn about gardening is to garden."

Perennials are grouped along the graceful fence which encloses a kitchen garden. An unusual feature of the stable building is its *pigeonnier*.

"It is not a large place: a plot of ground two hundred feet square would contain it. Houses surround it on three sides, while to the southwest, beyond the open lot of a neighbor, is the Ashley River. To reach the nearest woodland I must either traverse some two or three miles of city blocks, or else cross the river, which is here more than a mile wide. Actually in, and directly above, this garden I have seen one hundred and fourteen different species of birds. If, as is perfectly fair, I include those that I have seen from the window of the house, the number of species is one hundred and thirty-two—more than one third of the total number to be found in the entire state of South Carolina."

So wrote the well-known ornithologist Herbert Ravenel Sass in his 1911 article "Wild Life in a City Garden," which appeared in the *Atlantic Monthly*. Mr. Sass, whose family lived in the house for one hundred years before it was purchased by the present owners, Dr. and Mrs. H. R. Pratt-Thomas, would have been pleased to know that his garden still provides a refuge for human and wild occupants.

The design of the garden remains essentially the same as when it changed hands, but it has taken years of effort to tame the rampant bamboo that had grown up onto the porch, and years to establish some of the unusual specimens now thriving there. Entered from a long, private drive through stately early nineteenth-century wrought iron gates, the garden divides right and left, with the house dominating the formal hedge-enclosed lawn to the right, and a thicket of plants and trees surrounding a semi-circular lawn to the left. An enticing paved pathway weaves in and out of the plantings behind the south lawn, allowing close examination of specimens and access to a vegetable plot and a greenhouse filled with hundreds of orchids.

A goldfish pond provides an attractive focal point from the porch of the house and is occasionally also attractive to fishing birds and cats. One morning, no less than eleven egrets and herons were counted near the small pool.

By his own admission more of a horticulturalist than a gardener interested in overall design, Dr. Pratt-Thomas has collected an assortment of plants from all over, notably his camellias and orchids.

Many of the camellias were grown from seed or were grafted. Others, such as 'Pierate's Pride,' came from the destroyed garden at Pierate's Cruze in Mount Pleasant, South Carolina, or were prize acquisitions. Petal blight, however, has proven to be a serious, persistent problem that occurs every February, so Dr. Pratt-Thomas highly recommends assiduous care, as well as choosing early-blooming varieties. His favorites include: 'Marie Bracey,' 'Ville de Nantes,' 'Wildwood,' 'Mathotiana Supreme,' 'K. Sawada,' 'Guilio Nuccio,' The Sheffield family ('Betty,' 'Blush,' 'Supreme,' etc.), 'Rosea Superba,' 'C.M. Wilson,' 'Vulcan,' 'R.L. Wheeler,' and 'Elisabeth LeBay.'

Orchids are Dr. Pratt-Thomas's real passion. He likens his acquisition of a single orchid from Florida years ago to catching a disease, and notes that the receipt of *Orchid Digest* and other gardening magazines is an exciting event. For a while, the orchids lived in the bathtub, but became a minor nuisance there. With the aid of an assistant, a small greenhouse was constructed which has since grown to three rooms and provides unending diversion. During garden tours, the Pratt-Thomases delight in bringing out choice specimens for display. An enormous orchid, yellow dancing ladies (*Oncidium sphacelatum*), brought back from Caracas has over two hundred blooms in the spring and is a favorite with visitors. "We have orchids from Hawaii, Brazil, and all over," he indicates. "Actually, we have too many orchids, and I've just ordered four more."

In the garden, hardy local plants are combined with more unusual specimens such as a large cynoglossum (Chinese forget-me-not). Daylilies, declares the gardener, are prosaic, but most satisfactory.

Bearded iris abound because of their resemblance to orchids; cannas and aspidistra are deemed indestructible and therefore extremely useful. Hibiscus and the white French hydrangeas are favorites which have been propagated, and tall Queen Anne's lace comes back each year from seed.

An Englishman by birth, Dr. Pratt-Thomas inherited his love of plants from his mother, who was "a marvelous gardener." He used to follow her and help with seasonal plantings and has since gardened in every place he's lived. Although he has a particular fascination for unusual plants, it is the connection with friends and events in collecting plants which holds true enjoyment for him. "Gardening is a contact sport," he remarks, "and it's the association of those contacts and the flood of memories brought on by a plant's blossoming, for instance, that makes gardening such a personal delight."

Above: The main lawn and the house, seen from a path which winds throughout the garden. On the left is tall, airy, white Queen Anne's lace, which blooms in May.
Right: The entrance to the Robert Trail Chisolm garden, framed by early nineteenth-century wrought iron gates.

61

Top: A dwarf canna and blue salvia in front of the Virginia creeper, which turns a deep red in the fall. *Bottom:* Papyrus and water hyacinths in the goldfish pond.

Top: Crimson and yellow glory lilies (*Gloriosa Rothschildiana*). *Bottom:* A close-up view of orchids in the greenhouse.

An Eighteenth-Century Garden

Well-documented as being one of the earliest surviving gardens in the city, this pattern garden probably dates back to the 1790's, when it was laid out in the modified form of a fleur-de-lis. Originally edged with one-foot square red tiles, the beds presumably contained a variety of plants, as Peter Bocquet, the owner who commissioned the garden design, was reputedly interested in botany.

The beds contain interesting specimens today. The owner, an avid gardener, has recently replanted the parterres, aided by the suggestions of Reeser Manley, a horticultural instructor and landscape designer specializing in perennials. To achieve year-round bloom, the selection includes the old roses 'Will Scarlet' and 'Penelope,' yucca, cleomes, spiraea, lythrum 'Morden's Pink,' phlox, chrysanthemums, sedum 'Autumn Joy,' yellow *Iris pseudacorus*, veronica, purple coneflower (*Echinacea purpurea*), and the small white-flowered shrub *Serissa foetida*. Annuals are added seasonally. In the spring, Gerbera daisies, marigolds, geraniums, sweet allysum, and petunias are planted; late spring sees zinnias, purple ageratum (a favorite combination with yellow marigolds), shasta daisies, sweet William, and dianthus; fall is the time to plant stocks, calendulas, English daisies, dusty miller, snapdragons, and pansies.

The house has been in the owner's family since 1912, and pansies in the front beds along the wrought iron fence are a tradition fondly remembered by family and friends. "I grew up loving flowers and gardens," says the owner. "My mother was a wonderful gardener. She kept seventy-five rose bushes and grew beautiful flowers. I also had an aunt who was a member of a garden club which sponsored flower shows for children. My sister and I used to win ribbons. But holidays, especially Easter, are what I remember best in connection with the garden. My grandparents used to hide not just eggs, but baskets and presents in the flowerbeds. It was somewhat overgrown and jungle-like, but it was the memory of

Masses of annuals are planted by the owner throughout the year, with some reliance on perennials, such as the silver-grey artemisia in the middle foreground.

such lovely childhood days here that made me want to hold on to it—to tend the garden myself."

Even before the present family moved to the house in 1981, the garden restoration was underway. Loutrel Briggs had planted the beds prior to 1953. His plan was researched and implemented in part, but Briggs had relied heavily on herbs, which were not particularly successful this time. An enormous Lady

This design of one of the earliest extant pattern gardens in the city was probably laid out in the 1790's.

Banks rose was pruned up and its supporting trellis repaired. Numerous camellias and the stunning cycads known as sago palms were retained. Thousands of snowdrop and narcissus bulbs, which had naturalized out of bounds, were dug, as were hundreds of the tenacious cat's claw vines, some with bulbous roots the size of sweet potatoes.

"We discovered that most of the old red tiles were badly damaged, so we used brick dug up from the basement to redefine the borders," notes the owner. "My mother helped me garden every weekend for three years. I would get up at five A.M. in the summers to avoid the heat, and I installed the automatic watering system myself, with the help of our wonderful gardener, Joseph Weathers, who dug the trenches."

Joseph still helps tend the property, which also extends into a large lot behind the house and front garden. "I try to tell Joseph as much as I can about the plants and flowers, so he can answer questions from passers-by," remarks the owner, who says she seldom goes out to work that someone doesn't stop to com-

ment or ask questions. Partly for this reason, the front beds are frequently used for trials and unusual plants.

Most of the plantings have been trial-and-error since 1981, but in the spring of 1989, after realizing that a garden of largely annuals was simply too time-consuming, a wide variety of perennials were planted. These, too, are somewhat experimental at this stage, but the goal is to establish good border plants and ground covers which will help keep weeds down, and to enjoy the continuity and dependability of blooming plants that are successfully located.

"The tour buses slow down in front of our fence," tells the owner, "and tourists who pass by rejoice in our year-round growing season. I've enjoyed sending flowers to the museum houses, allowing a friend to pick for a wedding or a shower, and flowers from your own garden are always especially appreciated by someone in the hospital. I've always been interested in flower arranging and find myself very busy at holidays helping out. This sharing, with family, friends and the public, is really half the fun."

The Garden of the Benjamin Phillips House

Though relatively new, this totally enclosed garden has the look and feel of an earlier era. Extensive restoration of the 1818 house started in 1988, but there was no evidence of the original garden. The owners, Mr. and Mrs. John J. Avlon, sought the help of Hugh Dargan Associates, who were recommended on the basis of their expertise in historic preservation and design, in creating a garden that would be appropriate. The garden has been awarded the American Society of Landscape Architects' Merit Award for Design.

"I told the Dargans that I wanted the end result to be a charming eighteenth-century style garden, one with good 'bones' to it, yet nothing pretentious or grand," explains Mrs. Avlon. She felt that a naturalistic garden with winding paths and lawn was out of the question in such a limited area, and that one

with a lot of structure, especially architectural, was appealing.

A visit to the Charleston Museum's Heyward-Washington House, just a block up the street, was serendipitous; the back garden with its attractive parterres and dependencies provided inspiration.

A colonial privy at the museum house seemed the perfect answer for a garden building. The Avlon's property lent itself well to symmetry, so a pair of privies was constructed, complete with wooden doors and steep-pitched tile roofs. One building is useful for storing tools and irrigation machinery; the other serves as a potting shed. Shards of china, bits of oxidized glass, pipe stems, and other treasures unearthed during the garden excavation will be mortared into a mosaic inside one shed.

Recently completed by Hugh Dargan Associates, the pattern garden features symmetrical plantings of boxwood, hollies, camellias and azaleas.

The paved courtyard and formal garden in March.

Major problems had to be solved before any actual planting could begin. Footings for walls, wiring, and irrigation were established first. Drainage proved to be tricky; close to thirty bluestone drains were installed, and the area behind the house was elevated. Chain link fences and cinderblock boundary walls were replaced with new, old-style brick made in North Carolina, blending beautifully with the facade of a neighboring house along the drive.

From a design standpoint, there were angles in the property which needed visual correction before balance could be achieved. The parterre design was carefully drawn using hominy grits to show the proposed outlines. Old Charleston brick was located for the areas to be paved; the formal paths are of various crushed shells which blend into a medium gray color and which, unlike gravel, can be easily packed and neatly raked.

Mrs. Avlon's design philosophy is that the elements of such a garden should be simplified and few, but everything should be integrated, just as the proportions of a house can change from room to room yet relate as a whole. Her philosophy was expertly interpreted by the Dargans. A series of "rooms" for this garden begins with a long brick drive planted with anise and sasanquas, given privacy from the street by new wooden gates similar to others in the neighborhood. A second gate is smaller, scaled down in proportion with the garden beyond, and the wooden arch above it will eventually be covered with vines and climbing roses. A shaded terrace, accessible to porch and kitchen, brings the visitor around the corner of the house and leads into the formal rear garden featuring the parterres and privy buildings.

Plant material was selected to give a feeling of age, as well as to conform with Mrs. Avlon's ideas. "The only flowers I'd ever had were on chintz," she laughs. "My mother had a lovely garden, though, and her favorite blooms were largely pink and white." A similar palette was chosen here, and the Dargans were able to procure some large trees and shrubs, affecting an established look. A pair of Hume hollies, each weighing five-and-a-half tons with eight-foot diameter root balls, were expertly maneuvered into place against the back wall to shade a seating area. Four crape myrtles and four Foster hollies frame the central sundial garden. Crape myrtles were featured in a Russell

'Rosa Mundi' (*Rosa gallica versicolor*), the oldest of the striped roses, cultivated prior to 1581.

Page garden Mrs. Avlon had admired, and were an excellent choice here for summer bloom. Four old camellias, a pair of old-fashioned climbing roses, akebia vines, honeysuckles, and a pair of Zumi crabapples were also chosen. The Zumi variety of crabapple is a small tree featuring pink buds which open into white flowers which produce a berry-like fruit. Sasanquas were another choice, along with a double-flowering Madison jasmine which is cold-tolerant. Annuals are also chosen in pink and white shades. Outside the kitchen door are herbs for use in cooking.

Mrs. Avlon, who is a Master Gardener, has an interest in antique roses and has several varieties, including 'Cecile Brunner,' a polyantha, and 'Rosa Mundi' (*R. gallica versicolor*), the oldest striped rose on record.

The Florentine Craftsmen company in New York City was the source for the whimsical garden furniture, which features squirrels for arms on benches and chairs, and an acorn logo on each piece. A squirrel fountain was also custom designed in keeping with a statuary theme of small woodland animals.

Designing a garden with fine architectural features and a variety of interesting plant material is always an exciting project. Given the challenges of space, materials, and historic accuracy, the Dargans and the Avlons have combined talents to create a delightful addition to Charleston's historic district.

The rear facade of the house, seen through the garden in early spring. The moon gate in the background will eventually be covered with climbing roses.

Coral honeysuckle (*Lonicera sempervirens*) tangles around a sundial in the garden of the Benjamin Phillips house.

The entrance to the rear garden is framed by a pair of Zumi crabapples, whose red buds open into white flowers.

When Dr. Dwane Thomas purchased the property over ten years ago, the garden, which had been designed by Loutrel Briggs, had all but disappeared. Overly mature shrubs were beyond reshaping; copings and borders needed to be reset and outlines redefined. Dr. Thomas enlisted the help of interior designer, Allan Watkins, in reworking the garden and shaping its semi-formal appearance.

Entering the driveway alongside the residence, a long walkway leads past a former carriage house through an opening in a low, pierced brick wall. The wall serves not only as a visual introduction to the main garden, but also gives some privacy to the terrace immediately behind it. To the right, a renovated privy serves as a garden house. A rectangular lawn, neatly bordered with azaleas, camellias, and small trees in ascending height, terminates at a fountain designed by Mr. Watkins. The fountain and small

pool are of a particularly clever design: the dimensions are those of the notable wrought iron balcony on the street facade of the circa 1720 house.

Once practical considerations such as walkways, borders, and seating areas were established, new plant material needed to be purchased and existing plants tended, pruned, and shifted around. A neighbor gave sound advice to use what grows especially well in various Charleston gardens, so camellias, azaleas, nandinas, pittosporum, aucuba, ginger lilies, and a pomegranate tree were among the choices.

Studying the various approaches and seating areas in the garden, Mr. Watkins felt it was important to concentrate not just on the main vista of the garden, but also on vignettes, small compositions of plants, trees, pots and statuary to please the eye. Dwarf boxwoods frame beds of ground cover; a planter of trailing summer blooms is carefully placed at eye level on

The garden entrance, like so many now in Charleston, is through a parking area.

A terrace paved with flagstones overlooks the lawn, given privacy by a pierced brick wall draped with Confederate jasmine.

Although it is completely surrounded by city residences, there is a feeling of openness and space in the garden. The small pool at the end is scaled to the proportions of a fine iron balcony on the house.

a terminal wall; climbing plants are espaliered; and jasmine is arranged in swags on a low wall. Bloom comes largely from flowering shrubs and trees rather than beds of annuals or perennials, but maintenance is still high. Hybrid lantanas and jasmine need clipping twice a week in the warm months; the lawn is edged and mowed just as frequently.

Water gardening is a special pleasure. Dwarf lilies, iris, and papyrus grow well in the small pond, which is also inhabited by goldfish and snails. Other favorite aspects of the garden include plants which flourish in Charleston's sub-tropical climate. Dr. Thomas grows bougainvillea in large pots, yellow camellias propagated from a neighbor's plants, and a camphor tree (*Cinnamomum camphora*) from a seed that a friend sent from China. Visitors not familiar with our common pomegranates are delighted with the rosy, ancient fruits produced in the fall. Of particular importance and pleasure to Dr. Thomas is the ability to create "something pretty, charming, soothing—easy to look at." With the help of Mr. Watkins, Dr. Thomas has fashioned a garden that fits in beautifully with its surroundings, is a pleasure to the visitor, and has an individual character suited to its owner.

Pyracantha espaliered on a mellowed wall.

74

Dwarf water lilies, iris and papyrus fill this diminutive water garden. A custom-made heater keeps it viable through the winter months.

The Garden of the James Veree House

One of Charleston's most secluded and yet well-known gardens has been beautifully described by its owner in the book, *The American Woman's Garden.* This small, superb garden demonstrates a highly successful use of the long, narrow spaces which are frequently attached to older residences in Charleston. In her account of the garden, which is now nearly fifty years old, the owner described her goal "to plant the garden from front to back in seven sections—the three sections designed by Loutrel Briggs in 1942, and four additional sections that would challenge my imagination, my design ability, and my horticultural know-how."

She met the challenge of the thirty-by-fifty foot space with a flair. Presently able to devote time daily to gardening chores and pleasures, she recalls earlier days of achieving her planting goals area by area, as the children's needs changed and the budget allowed. Now particularly glorious in the spring, the garden's basic design has long been complete, but its elements are dynamic.

A narrow, shady passage opens onto a winding flagstone path beyond a small terrace, bringing the vista, which sweeps the length of the space, into view. Wide borders of perennials, annuals, and background shrubs gaily articulate the length of the oval lawn, then give way to clipped boxwoods and a low retaining wall encircling a round lawn and reflecting pond. Beyond this circular area lies a slightly raised second terrace of old brick, which is largely shaded,

The reflecting pond designed by landscape architect, Loutrel Briggs, is only an inch deep, but adds a great deal of visual depth to the garden.

A scalloped fence is a pretty background for this lavishly planted late spring border.

A close-up view of the reflecting pond. In the background, at the end of the terrace, is a rocky pool with a tiny trickling waterfall.

One of several charming birdbaths found in the garden, here tucked in among the annuals and perennials.

its edges defined by azaleas, camellias, and hydrangeas. Drawn further into the space, the visitor notices and hears a trickling stream ending in a tiny pool surrounded by a variety of rocks and coral interplanted with violets, trillium, and ginger. Nearby, and nearly hidden by the dense shrubbery, a sloping path veers to the right, then turns sharply into a narrow lane behind azaleas along the property line. Here, another miniature waterfall is revealed, guarded by three stone foxes. Other small animal sculptures are tucked in among hostas, ferns, and ground covers, adding elements of surprise and discovery. This woodland atmosphere also creates an unexpected change of mood from the formal garden preceding it.

The owner prefers structure in a garden and feels that it is particularly vital in a small garden. She points out that much of her garden's interest lies in the fact that there are both narrow and wide areas, sunny as well as shady spots, and a slight change in elevation. Buckets of rich earth were hauled in to build up the far end, providing a slope for water and added height for the azaleas. She notes that rearranging the changing plant material is part of the fun of gardening, while judicious and regular pruning is a must.

Professing that she's really "just a farmer," the owner comes from a family with a long tradition of gardening. "I now am learning to be more of a horticulturalist and am interested in what I can do to the environment to produce the best results," she says.

"I like collections of plants, and I like for plantings to make a statement. Over time, my eye for color and shape has become more cultivated, more sophisticated. White is particularly useful in the garden—I think it really sparkles. Experimenting with new plants and combinations is fun, but if something needs too much fussing and nursing, out it goes. Gardeners have to rely upon the really tough plants, the workhorses. For example, I have ten floribunda 'Sunflare' roses, which are prolific bloomers and fairly disease resistant."

"Balance and symmetry are most important," she continues, "but can be difficult to achieve. Just as one of a pair of something is perfect, the other will succumb to any number of troubles. For example, needing a pair of azaleas at the entrance to the far terrace which would bloom at exactly the same time, I cut an enormous one in half, and they still don't bloom simultaneously."

As for advice to the would-be gardeners, this experienced gardener says, "Don't feel you have to rush into everything at once. Plan your garden in stages; you'll learn and learn, and you'll get to know each plant. I have actually developed a one-on-one relationship with each of my plants—a co-dependence, if you will—and my enjoyment of the whole endeavor has deepened and broadened. It has brought much expected treasure and many unexpected friends. You know, a friend once remarked to me, 'That garden has become a part of your life.' And so it has."

Afternoon shade falls across a border filled with a variety of annuals and perennials, including phlox, nicotiana, dahlias and coreopsis.

A favorite of tourists, photographers, artists, and residents is the picturesque street facade of the circa 1800 Timothy Ford House, the home of Dr. and Mrs. A. Bert Pruitt. In early spring, the wrought iron fence of the garden is nearly hidden by a magnificent drapery of lavender wisteria racemes, set off against the formal white Federal house and the low white stucco wall beneath.

A series of individual gardens, each with a different theme, progresses alongside the house toward the raised formal beds at the rear of the property. In the front garden, six Kwanzan cherries are evenly spaced around an oval lawn separated from another lawn by a bricked-in terrace. The terrace contains a central bed of rosemary and two circular rose beds, surrounded by semi-annual blooming 'fashion' azaleas and eight crape myrtles. An enormous elm overshadows the second lawn, providing a canopy of high filtered shade. Two more pairs of cherries continue the sequence, with an abundant variety of well-tended camellias. To the right, a wooden summerhouse adorned with a Lady Banks rose is approached by a corridor of boxwoods. Yew hedges flank a wide, mossy step leading up into a topiary garden of clipped box and holly featuring a fountain against the terminal wall. Azaleas are repeated in the peripheral planting. Four huge camellia trees accent the corners, and stone benches invite contemplative rest.

When the Pruitts acquired the property in 1969, the garden had become overgrown and lacked balance. A sunken garden, since replaced by a boxwood walk, was frequently full of stagnant water following heavy rains. Loutrel Briggs had designed the back garden with double rows of peach trees for the approach, but disease and age had taken their toll.

Mr. Briggs was consulted again in 1975, but his design was altered. Around this time, the Pruitts had been given a copy of Rosemary Verey's book, *The English Woman's Garden*. In it was a garden that captivated Dr. Pruitt and inspired him to write for permission to copy a rose-covered structure from one of the photographs. In reply, he received a lovely note from the Duchess of Beaufort saying that she was flattered, and so was Russell Page, who had done the original drawings.

A local lumberyard built the "folly," which turned out to be sixteen feet across and impossible to maneuver either up or over the fence, or down the alley leading to the back gates. So it was taken apart and reassembled just a few yards away.

Plantings were completed in stages because the lawns served as open warehouses for heart-pine flooring and other construction materials during major restoration of the house. Ultimately, a bulldozer was brought in for leveling twenty-four truckloads of soil and for moving some of the larger established trees and shrubs, heeled-in until they could be placed properly.

Although Mr. Briggs was consulted on several more occasions, part of the overall design occurred by chance. A nursery low on dogwoods had a special on cherry trees; some of the crape myrtles left over from the set of a movie filmed on the premises were planted. A number of plants came from a large nursery owned by Mrs. Pruitt's family.

Dr. Pruitt, frustrated by a lack of cooperation from brick-masons, took a course in brick-laying and put down the terrace by himself. The terrace works well for entertaining, as a large round table covers the central bed nicely and a tent for dancing is easily set up over a paved parking area outside the back gates. Lighting was carefully planned.

Although there is no greenhouse, two enclosed porch spaces serve this need. A recent glance inside revealed over thirty young camellias, including 'Borum's Gem,' named for a well-known local grower; 'Tomcat,' a particularly vivid red; a variegated 'Betty Sheffield Supreme;' and the showy pale pink 'Mrs. D.W. Davis.'

The Pruitts receive pleasure from their classic garden through all the seasons. "Our calendar is the garden," says Mrs. Pruitt, "and we enjoy every minute of it."

This garden is a cool tapestry of textures in June. Clipped boxwood, holly and yew provide form and background for a variety of azaleas and camellias.

A rose-covered gazebo based on a Russell Page design, by permission of the Duchess of Beaufort.

82

Above: The front garden in spring. *Below:* The facade of the Timothy Ford house, with its wisteria-laden fence.

83

A Garden in Ansonborough

Dating from about 1836, the Greek Revival house on a quiet street was in a state of disrepair when Mr. and Mrs. Lawrence Walker purchased the property in 1973. The large zigzag lot around it was choked with weeds and crowded with cherry laurels, thick oleander bushes, and overgrown althea.

Once the lot had been cleared and an enormous, sun-stealing pecan tree removed, the Walkers began plotting designs. Both were experienced gardeners, and they had owned Mulberry Plantation in nearby Berkeley County for several years, where they had maintained the extensive gardens designed by Loutrel Briggs.

The space on Laurens Street seemed to lend itself well to a series of garden "rooms" on different levels. At the back of the lot, a raised terrace and swimming pool were put in. Directly behind the house, a courtyard was paved with bricks found on the property. Part of the same courtyard was designated the private domain of the carriage house by surrounding an area with a low wall, a wrought iron fence, and high-pruned wax myrtles. The house sits on the eastern side of the lot, and the main garden lies to the west. Here, the Walkers laid hoses in a free-form pattern of curves to help design the borders, which could be seen from the porch. At the south end of this garden, below the three-story brick facade of a neighboring house, a small formal area with boxwood parterres and crushed shell walkways was planted.

Complementing the wooden house, dark green picket fences surround the front garden. Against its western fence, camphor trees were chosen to alternate with wax myrtles. Evergreen cleyera and hollies helped complete a privacy screen, and dogwood trees were transplanted from a former garden in Summerville. The dogwoods add fall and winter interest, while their showy white spring blossoms balance the deep corals and pinks of numerous 'Pride of Summerville' and other azalea varieties planted in the wide beds. Variegated pittosporum is used to brighten shady areas; liriope is a reliable, hardy border. A large iris collection is another feature, and there are several delightful modern and classical garden ornaments.

"The pool area is our summer garden," says Mrs. Walker. Here, a wooden trellis supports well-pruned kiwi vines which produce excellent fruit. The vines also protect a terrace from summer sun. To the east

Carolina jessamine in front of the house.

Pansies, candytuft and scilla are planted in drifts along the front borders of curving beds.

Conical boxwoods mark the steps leading into the formal rose garden.

Trelliswork screens the greenhouse and supports the tropical yellow vine *Allamanda cathartica*. Zinnias and blue plumbago provide additional color.

of the pool, an eight-foot lattice screen hides a greenhouse and work area. In late spring, pots of a yellow tropical vine (*Allamanda cathartica*) are brought out from the greenhouse, along with the pink tropical mandevilla, and are encouraged to sprawl along the lattice. Perennial pale blue plumbago fills in the area at the base of the vines. Clivia and orchids are brought out as well.

Another bed around the pool contains a collection of multi-colored ginger lilies, including *Hedychium coronarium* (white), *H. flavescens* (yellow), *H. Gardneranum* (yellow), *H. coccineum* (red), and *H. villosum* (white). More exotics, including papyrus and banana trees, come back after dying down each winter. The Walkers tried growing sweet red grapes along the west pool wall for a while, but the vines did not do well in Charleston's high humidity.

Summer sun is welcome in the raised rose bed between the front garden and the pool, while a young live oak planted nearby shades part of the brick

courtyard and the carriage house in the afternoons. In addition to hybrid tea roses, there are several Lady Banks roses which climb and drape prettily over brick cornices. Carolina jessamine and a hardy California jasmine add more touches of yellow in spring and summer. A Japanese maple, kept in scale with annual pruning, turns a deep red in the fall.

Other successful plantings include a long row of clipped nandina bushes along a semi-shaded walk and a wide bed of mondo grass used as groundcover. Full of exotic or unusual specimens, as well as many of the native and hardy plants frequently seen in the city, the garden offers a great deal of year-round interest. Even in the dead of winter, one can admire the neat, clipped forms of box and holly, the pale bark of bare kiwi vines against their dark supports, berries on nandina and holly, or the light on one of the whimsical bird sculptures by Charles Smith, which are placed in the garden.

87

The best way to see the gardens and houses of Charleston is on foot, although the elevation afforded on a carriage ride may allow for occasional glimpses over walls and privacy hedges. Exploring the peninsula on an unhurried walk is a delightful way to spend several hours in the early morning and late afternoon. The light in Charleston can have a magical quality, but a rainy day will bring out the faded colors of painted stucco and the full range of greens in the gardens. An overcast day provides a good opportunity for garden photography.

The gardens vary considerably, of course, but here are a few rough guidelines to keep in mind: for the most part, the largest private city gardens are attached to the grand houses on Meeting Street, Legare Street, and South Battery. Along East Bay Street and Charleston's popular Rainbow Row, the lots are often long and narrow. Queen Street, King Street, Church Street, and Tradd Street are famous for their architecture, and for an exciting variety of gardens, handsome walls and gates, and stunning ironwork. Charming cobbled alleys and narrow ways are often shady, presenting a challenge to the determined gardener, frequently with picturesque results.

The City of Charleston has an excellent landscape team, and the visitor will certainly enjoy Washington Park, White Point Gardens, the Battery, Waterfront

Park, Hampton Park, and Cypress Gardens, northeast of Charleston. The gardens of the Charleston Museum and Historic Charleston Foundation's historic houses are superb and should not be missed.

Finally, the world-famous Middleton Place and Magnolia Gardens are only a short drive from the city on Ashley River Road.

Left: Colorful floral accents on Tradd Street. *Above:* A garden path leads past a "dependency" and beds of scilla. *Top right:* A glimpse into a walled garden on Church Street. *Bottom right:* A perennial border on Beaufain Street.

Top: Ground orchid (bletilla), snowdrops and ranunculas cover the base of a birdbath. *Bottom:* A small pond displays a variety of water plants, including lilies and lotus.

A peppermint peach in front of the Judge Robert Pringle house downtown.

Suggested Reading

Briggs, Loutrel W. *Charleston Gardens*. Columbia: University of South Carolina Press, 1951.

Halfacre, R. Gordon and Shawcroft, Anne R. *Carolina Landscape Plants*. Raleigh: Sparks Press, 1975.

Halfacre, R. Gordon and Shawcroft, Anne R. *Landscape Plants of the Southeast*. Raleigh: Sparks Press, 1971.

Hunt, William Lanier. *Southern Gardens, Southern Gardening*. Durham: Duke University Press, 1982.

Lawrence, Elizabeth. *Gardening For Love, The Market Bulletins*. Durham: Duke University Press, 1986.

Page, Russell. *The Education of a Gardener*. New York: Random House, 1985.

Perenyi, Eleanor. *Green Thoughts: A Writer in the Garden*. New York: Random House, 1981.

Schenck, George. *The Complete Shade Gardener*. Boston: Houghton Mifflin Company, 1984.

The Garden Club of Charleston. *The Gardeners' Guide for Charleston and the Low Country*. Rev. ed., Charleston: The Garden Club of Charleston, 1990.

Trustees Garden Club of Savannah, Georgia. *Garden Guide to the Lower South*. Memphis: Wimmer Brothers, 1986.

Verey, Rosemary and Samuels, Ellen. *The American Woman's Garden*. Boston: Little, Brown & Company, 1984.

Verey, Rosemary. *The Garden In Winter*. Boston: Little, Brown & Company, 1968.

Welch, William C. *Perennial Garden Color For Texas and The South*. Dallas: Taylor Publishing Company, 1989.

Botanical Nomenclature

A Listing of Many of the Plant Materials Found in Charleston Gardens

BOTANICAL NAME	COMMON NAME	BOTANICAL NAME	COMMON NAME
Acer	Maple	*Cleyera japonica*	Cleyera
Adiantum	Maidenhair Fern	*Cornus florida*	Flowering Dogwood
Agapanthus africanus	Lily of the Nile	*Crinum*	Crinum Lily
Ajuga reptans	Bugleweed; Carpet Bugle	*Cunninghamia*	China Fir
Akebia quinata	Chocolate Vine	*X Cupressocyparis Leylandii*	Leyland Cypress
Albizia julibrissin	Mimosa: Silk Tree	*Cycas revoluta*	Sago Palm
Althaea officinalis	Marsh Mallow	*Cyperus Papyrus*	Papyrus
Alyssum	Carpet of Snow	*Cyrtomium falcatum*	Holly Fern
Amaryllis	Amaryllis		
Anthemis	Chamomile	*Daphne odora*	Winter Daphne
Antirrhinum majus	Snapdragon	*Dianthus barbatus*	Sweet William
Aquilegia	Columbine	*Dianthus Caryopyllus*	Carnation, Clove Pink
Arundinaria	Bamboo	*Digitalis*	Foxglove
Asparagus densiflorus 'Sprengeri'	Asparagus Fern; Emerald Fern	*Diospyros*	Persimmon
Aspidistra elatior	Cast-iron plant	*Eleagnus*	Eleagnus
Aucuba japonica	Japanese Laurel; Gold-dust Tree	*Eriobotrya japonica*	Loquat, Japanese Plum
		Euonymus	Spindle Tree
Azalea, see Rhododendron			
		X Fatshedera Lizei	Tree Ivy
Begonia	Begonia	*Fatsia japonica*	Fatsia; Japanese Fatsia
Betula nigra	River Birch	*Ficus carica*	Common Fig
Buddleia	Butterfly Bush	*Ficus pumila*	Fig Vine; Creeping Fig
Buxus sempervirens	Boxwood	*Fortunella*	Kumquat
		Franklinia Alatamaha	Franklin Tree; Gordonia
Caladium bicolor	Caladium		
Camellia japonica	Camellia	*Gamolepis chrysanthemoides*	African Shrub Daisy
Camellia sasanqua	Sasanqua Camellia	*Gardenia jasminoides*	Gardenia
Camellia sinensis	Tea plant	*Gelsemium sempervirens*	Carolina Yellow Jessamine
Campsis radicans	Trumpet Vine		
Canna indica	Indian-Shot	*Gerbera Jamesoni*	Transvaal Daisy; African Daisy
Cedrus	Cedar		
Celtis	Hackberry; Sugarberry Tree	*Ginkgo biloba*	Ginkgo Tree; Maidenhair Tree
Chaenomeles speciosa	Japanese Quince	*Gordonia Lasianthus*	Loblolly Bay; Black Laurel
Chrysanthemum	Chrysanthemum		
Chrysanthemum x superbum	Shasta Daisy	*Gypsophila elegans*	Baby's Breath
Cinnamomum camphora	Camphor Tree		
Clematis Armandii	Armand Clematis	*Hedera helix*	English Ivy
Clerodendrum Thomsoniae	Bleeding-Heart Vine	*Hedychium coronarium*	Ginger Lily

95

BOTANICAL NAME	COMMON NAME	BOTANICAL NAME	COMMON NAME
Hemerocallis	Daylily	*Butia*	Cocos Palm
Hibiscus Syriacus	Rose of Sharon	*Butia capitata*	Jelly Palm
Hosta	Hosta; Plantain-lily	*Jubaea chilensis*	Honey Palm
Hyacinthus orientalis	Common Hyacinth	*Livistona chinensis*	Chinese Fan Palm
Hydrangea	Hydrangea	*Phoenix*	Date Palm
		Rhapidophyllum hystrix	Porcupine Palm
Iberis sempervirens	Candytuft	*Sabal causiarum*	Puerto Rican Hat Palm
Ilex opaca	American Holly	*Sabal palmetto*	Cabbage Palmetto
Ilex vomitoria	Yaupon Holly; Cassina	*Trachycarpus Fortunei*	Windmill Hemp Palm
Illicium floridanum	Anise	*Parkinsonia aculeata*	Jerusalem Thorn
Impatiens wallerana	Impatiens; Patient Lily	*Parthenocissus quinquefolia*	Virginia Creeper
Ipomoea	Morning-Glory	*Pelargonium*	Geranium
Iris x germanica	Flag; Bearded Iris	*Phlox paniculata*	Perennial Phlox
Iris hollandica	Dutch Iris	*Photinia*	Photinia; Red Tip
		Pittosporum	Pittosporum
Justicia Brandegeana	Shrimp Plant	*Plumbago auriculata*	Cape Leadwort
		Podocarpus macrophyllus	Southern Yew
Lagerstroemia indica	Crape Myrtle	*Prunus caroliniana*	Cherry Laurel
Lantana camara	Lantana; Yellow Sage	*Prunus Persica*	Peach
Leucojum vernum	Spring Snowflake	*Punica Granatum*	Pomegranate
Ligustrum	Privet	*Pyracantha*	Pyracantha; Firethorn
Liriope	Lily Turf	*Pyrus Calleryana 'Bradford'*	Bradford Pear
Lobularia maritima	Sweet Alyssum		
Lonicera	Honeysuckle	*Quercus virginiana*	Live Oak
Loropetalum	Loropetalum		
Lycoris radiata	Spider Lily	*Raphiolepis indica*	Indian Hawthorn
Lycoris squamigera	Magic Lily;	*Rhododendron*	Azalea
	Resurrection Lily	*Rosa banksiae*	Lady Banks Rose
		Rosa laevigata	Cherokee Rose
Magnolia grandiflora	Southern Magnolia		
Magnolia x soulangiana	Tulip Tree	*Saxifraga stolonifera*	Strawberry Begonia
Mahonia	Oregon Grape, Holly Grape	*Serissa foetida*	Serissa
Malus augustifolia	Southern Crab Apple	*Spiraea*	Bridal Wreath
Matthiola incana	Stock	*Stokesia laevis*	Stokes Aster
Michelia Figo	Banana Shrub		
Musa x paradisiaca	Banana	*Tetrapanex papyriferus*	Chinese Rice—Paper Plant
Myrica cerifera	Wax Myrtle	*Tillandsia usneoides*	Spanish Moss
		Trachelospermum asiaticum	Japanese Star Jasmine
Nandina domestica	Nandina; Heavenly Bamboo	*Trachelospermum jasminoides*	Confederate Jasmine
Nerium oleander	Common Oleander		
		Viburnum odoratissimum	Sweet Viburnum
Ophiopogon	Mondo grass; Lily Turf	*Vinca Minor*	Common Periwinkle
Osmanthus fragrans	Tea Olive	*Vitex Agnus-castus*	Chaste Tree
Palmae	Palms	*Wisteria sinensis*	Chinese Wisteria
Acrocomia	Gru-Gru Palm		

The source for the above terms is *Hortus Third*, by Liberty Hyde Bailey and Ethel Joe Bailey.
New York: MacMillan Publishing Company, 1976.